1981

Educational Research Series No. 60

The Role of Grammar
in a Secondary School
Curriculum

The Role of Grammar in a Secondary School Curriculum

W. B. Elley, I. H. Barham,
H. Lamb and M. Wyllie

New Zealand Council
for Educational Research
Wellington, 1979

New Zealand Council
for Educational Research
P.O. Box 3237, Wellington

© NZCER 1979

ISBN 0-908567-09-X

Printed by
Whitcoulls Limited
561 Colombo Street
Christchurch

Foreword

Aorere College, the venue for this study, was established in 1964. The period since then has been one of continuing change in the field of secondary education in New Zealand. Many traditional approaches have been re-examined not only in curriculum but also in the organization and functioning of schools. During such a time a school's attitude towards change is a critical factor in its progress. At one extreme the school can try to ignore or resist pressures for change and cling closely to the familiar patterns of the past. At the other extreme it can seize eagerly on new ideas as they emerge and literally jump aboard the current band waggon without serious thought as to what the consequences will be.

A more sensible approach is carefully and seriously to examine any proposal for change, to find out what it involves, and what effects it would have on the school and its pupils. Aorere College adopted this approach with regard both to curriculum changes, and to other key developments, such as the provision of guidance, the establishment of closer school-community relationships and the grouping of pupils for a variety of purposes.

During 1968-69 two members of the Aorere staff, Ian Barham and Malcolm Wyllie, attended a series of lectures sponsored by the Auckland English Association on alternative approaches to the teaching of English. The lively discussions that followed these lectures gave rise to certain basic questions about the role of grammar and other topics in the English curriculum. As a foundation member of staff, Ian Barham had already made a major contribution to the planning and development of the school as well as building up a strong English department. It is worth noting, too, that before joining the Aorere staff he had been associated with the New Zealand Council for Educational Research for a year as the holder of the J. R. McKenzie Fellowship. Together with Malcolm Wyllie he now approached the Council seeking its assistance, on behalf of the school, to carry out a research study of the problem.

By coincidence, the Council had received a formal request from a review committee of the New English Syllabus Committee (NESC) to investigate the contribution that formal grammar makes to the English programme. Consequently, the Council asked its Assistant Director, Warwick Elley, a former teacher of English, to join Ian Barham and Malcolm Wyllie in planning and implementing a three-year research project. Dr Elley provided the expertise, particularly with the task of evaluation, and became a regular visitor to the school. They were joined by Hilary Lamb, a very able and imaginative young teacher. The group worked extremely well as a team, and because they were held in high regard as individuals they gained the ready cooperation of other members of staff. The Director of Secondary Education allocated a special time allowance for the staff participating in the project, and over the three years other teachers of English in a number of Auckland secondary schools gave dedicated assistance with the marking of pupils' essays.

The results of the experiment were first published in the *New Zealand Journal of Educational Research* Vol. 10, No. 1, 1975. The significance of the conclusions attracted much attention, and the article was later re-published, by permission, in the American journal, *Research in the Teaching of English*. Continued requests for more information prompted NZCER to publish this full monograph.

We at Aorere College were pleased to have been associated with the Council in this project. One would hope that in the future there will be other occasions when a school will engage in partnership with NZCER to investigate important areas of New Zealand education.

CHARLES M. HERBERT
Former Principal
Aorere College

January 1979

Contents

List of Tables

List of Figures

1

Introduction: What is the Role of English Grammar?

> A student motivated to improve his writing will find a conscious understanding of the syntax an obvious help. For many students it is an indispensable one.
>
> P. Roberts[1]

> Grammar not merely has a use in the English class-room, but is indispensable. ... It is not, and never should be taught as an end in itself. Its value is that it provides part of the technique for good writing.
>
> I. A. Gordon[2]

Generations of teachers of English language have been schooled against a background of faith in the undoubted benefits of instruction in formal grammar. Textbooks, curriculum outlines, examination papers and prestigious writers on English in each period provide ample testimony to the confidence placed in grammar as a prerequisite to good writing, and as an invaluable mental discipline, a necessary preparation for learning foreign languages, and a convenient method of introducing the student to new language structures.

More recently, however, the tide has begun to turn. Sceptics have been prone to argue that, if grammar is so important for a child's intellectual and linguistic development, its benefits should be reflected in his written work. Yet, 60 years of empirical research studies on the practical value of teaching traditional grammar have failed to demonstrate that it does

1. P. Roberts, *English Syntax* (New York: Harcourt Brace, 1964).
2. I. A. Gordon, *The Teaching of English* (Wellington: NZCER, 1947).

produce dramatic effects. Most studies have shown no benefits at all. Doubts have lingered, however, about the conclusiveness of these findings, and it is true that many investigations do not bear close scrutiny. Inevitably, a proper study of the potential, and side effects, of an extended course in language study is more complex than it seems, and few researchers have been meticulous enough to carry it out over a sufficiently long period with the required rigour. Despite these caveats, the fact remains that proponents of the cause of grammar have been disappointed in their search for evidence which attests to its practical worth.

Grammar teachers have been on the defensive for other reasons too. The impact of psychological insights on the importance of interest and motivation in learning, on the slow development of abstract thinking in children, and on the apparent lack of transfer of logical thinking skills to practical situations has raised doubts in the minds of many thoughtful English teachers about the wisdom of stressing syntax. And the appearance of new grammars (structural and transformational), which claim to describe language production more accurately than the prescriptions of traditional grammar, have served often to confuse, if not to undermine, the practising teacher, content in his beliefs. In the absence of definite knowledge and authoritative consensus, what is he to accept? Has grammar an important place in the crowded curriculum at all? If so, which type? How and when should it be taught? What contribution does it make? What else must be sacrificed?

We do not presume that this concern is the major preoccupation of secondary school English teachers. In the past half century, debate has been accelerating on many aspects of English—the proper objectives, content, and methods of teaching; the priorities for oral and written work; the importance of instruction in reading and listening skills; the place of the new media; and the purpose of literature teaching—to name a few of the major concerns. Nevertheless, the value of grammar is a regular topic for heated debate, in newspapers, in school staffrooms and in parent-teacher meetings. As new syllabuses are framed, decisions have to be made by curriculum planners on the proper place to assign to it. And this is one question on which research can be expected to shed some light.

Traditional teachers in New Zealand and elsewhere have clung to formal grammar for a variety of reasons. Defenders of the faith, such as Professor Gordon,[3] justified grammar because it gives pupil and teacher 'a common technical vocabulary' and 'provides the teacher with a reservoir of illustrative material which is there at call if the need for illustration arises'. The American report on *Freedom and Discipline in English*[4] dwelt on the value of grammar as an aid in eradicating faults, as a basis for communication between teacher and student, and as an important guide to the pattern and orderliness of language. Phoebe Meikle expressed regret that the discrediting of grammar constitutes a serious threat to language because

---

3. I. A. Gordon, *op. cit.*

4. Report of the Commission on English, *Freedom and Discipline in English* (New York: College Entrance Examinations Board, 1965).

of the inevitable 'vagueness and ambiguity' which will ensue.[5] And in recent years, campaigners for the 'Back to Basics' movement in education around the Western World are advocating strong doses of English grammar as a cure for some of our educational ills.

Some modern linguists have made similar claims for the new descriptive grammars, and new textbooks are frequently produced on the assumption that they will assist the student in practical ways with his writing. But the more cautious linguist is now retreating to a position which claims that linguistics need no justification. Paul Roberts[6] claims that language should be studied 'objectively and dispassionately, for its own sake'. Others argue that it is 'part of a genuinely liberal education', 'an important thing to know', or 'a means to an enlightened understanding of how our language system works'.

The question for the English teacher is whether, in an increasingly congested curriculum, he can afford the time to dwell on a subject which has seldom captured the imagination of the student, and which will necessarily supplant other language activities which may well do so. For how many students is the argument that linguistic knowledge is its own reward a sufficient justification for sacrificing growth in other language activities?

Critics of the traditional approach argue that the defence of grammar is a mere rationalization for the desire to avoid change and to cling to a secure clearly-sequenced course, easy to teach and easy to test. This claim may have some truth, but it is now clear that large numbers of New Zealand teachers have deliberately abandoned the teaching of grammar altogether, and now place their faith in 'naturalistic' approaches to the teaching of communication skills, through wide reading, dramatic activities, extensive writing, and informal discussion of the students' own productions. Others again, have turned to new grammars, such as the Oregon Curriculum's transformational grammar, or Halliday's approach, as represented in the grammar produced by Scott, Bowley, Brocket, Brown and Goddard.[7] Meanwhile the direction of liberal thinking, as represented in recent in-service courses in English and the proposals of the New English Syllabus Committee (NESC),[8] is clear. As the emphasis on 'oracy' and the new media increases, so the emphasis on traditional studies, such as formal grammar, will perforce decline correspondingly.

Clearly the English teacher needs guidance. In the absence of definite knowledge about the probable utilitarian or humanitarian values of grammar, it is difficult for him to decide whether, how much, and what kind of grammar to teach to whom. The authors of this project set out to investigate these issues.

---

5. P. Meikle, *School and Nation: Post-Primary Education since the War* (Wellington: NZCER, 1961).

6. P. Roberts, 'The Relation of Linguistics to the Teaching of English', in *College English*, vol. 22 pp. 7–8, 1960.

7. F. S. Scott, C. C. Bowley, C. S. Brocket, J. G. Brown and P. R. Goddard, *English Grammar* (Auckland: Heinemann, 1968).

8. NESC, *Statement of Aims* (Wellington: Department of Education, 1978).

New Developments in Linguistics

The advances of knowledge about language and linguistics in the past two or three decades have been dramatic. The rise to prominence of the structural grammars of Fries[9] and Trager and Smith[10] was quickly followed by the rival models of the transformational-generative grammar of Chomsky[11] and the neo-Firthian categorial grammars of Halliday[12] and his British colleagues.

Both the traditional and the new 'scientific' grammars attempt to reveal the way the language is put together and the way it works. But, whereas traditional grammar has tended to be prescriptive, the approach taken by scientific linguists is basically descriptive. The latter deliberately avoid value judgements or recommended practices and concentrate on describing language as a form of behaviour.

The structuralist, for instance, makes careful observations of language in action and attempts to draw inductive conclusions about its structure. To do this he studies phonemes and morphemes and the way in which these elements are combined to form words, phrases and sentences, and so tries to explain the system by which we communicate meaning. The transformational-generative grammarian also concentrates on description of language use, but his approach is more deductive than that of the structuralist. He starts with a theory of basic underlying elements, which users of language are intuitively able to modify or transform with the aid of identifiable rules to generate new sentences. He makes predictions about language behaviour from his knowledge of these transformational rules and tests them against the forms we actually see. Also, he argues that the structure of sentences cannot be understood without considering their meaning; the structuralist, by contrast, attempts to divorce his analyses from the meanings of the words he studies. Other methods of linguistic analysis have also emerged in the past two decades, the most notable being tagnemics and case grammar, but these have had less impact on classroom English teaching.

This is not the place to detail or evaluate the claims of these new grammars. More information on transformational grammar is contained in Chapter 4, and we must not prejudge our case by evaluating the system before we have studied the empirical evidence. However, it is important to realize at the outset that these grammar systems are sufficiently different from traditional grammar to reopen the question of the pedagogical value of a study of scientific grammars, quite apart from the value of their more traditional forerunners.

As a result of such developments in linguistics, many new curricula

9. C. C. Fries, *The Structure of English* (New York: Harcourt Brace, 1952).

10. G. L. Trager and H. L. Smith, 'An Outline of English Structure', in *Studies in Linguistics Occasional Papers*, No. 3 (Washington, D.C.: American Council of Learned Societies, 1951).

11. N. Chomsky, *Syntactic Structures* (The Hague: Mouton, 1957).

12. M. A. K. Halliday et al., *The Linguistic Sciences and Language Teaching* (London: Longmans, Green, 1964).

were evolved in the United States and Great Britain during the 1960s. Among these was the *Oregon Curriculum*[13] which deliberately set out to apply Jerome Bruner's concepts of 'structure' in knowledge, and 'the spiral curriculum', to the study of English. This curriculum is composed of three separate 'strands', one of which is largely devoted to a systematic course in transformational grammar, inspired by the ideas of Noam Chomsky.

The Oregon Curriculum was considered to be eminently suitable for use in the present investigation, not only because it included a carefully developed course in a modern grammar, but also because the three-strand nature of the curriculum would make it easier to examine more clearly the effects of studying such a grammar. Thus, matched groups of pupils could be identified, and, while some pupils were studying the formal language strand, the others would undertake different studies, completely unrelated to grammar.

After discussion with Dr Kitzhaber, the General Editor of the Oregon Curriculum, a third group of pupils was included in the investigation, to undertake a course in English of the kind often found in New Zealand secondary schools at the time of the investigation. This addition enabled a comparison to be made between the Oregon Curriculum as a whole and a more traditional course, and provided a broader framework for an evaluation of each.

It was fortunate that the organization of the school in which the study took place lent itself well to the demands of the investigation. The third form intake was normally divided into three broad levels of ability, the middle one being a large group of pupils of average ability who could be divided into eight matched and relatively homogeneous classes. This organization was able to be sustained for three years, without disrupting the school unduly.

Main Purposes

Thus, the major purpose of this research project was to investigate the effects on the language development of secondary school pupils of a study of transformational grammar as represented in the Oregon English Curriculum. The investigation was carried out, over a period of three years, by comparing the growth in a number of language skills of pupils who made a regular study of the Oregon Curriculum, including the transformational grammar 'strand', with that of pupils who studied the Oregon Curriculum without this strand. The aspects of language on which the growth of pupils was compared included essay writing, sentence structure, usage, spelling, reading comprehension, vocabulary, literature and attitudes. Details of the areas and techniques of evaluation are to be found in Chapter 6.

13. A. R. Kitzhaber, ed., *The Oregon Curriculum. A Sequential Program in English* (New York: Holt, Rinehart & Winston, 1970).

B

Other subsidiary purposes of the project were:

(1) to evaluate the Oregon Curriculum as a whole.
(2) to evaluate a more traditional type of English programme based on a widely used New Zealand textbook series, *Let's Learn English*, by **P. R.** Smart.

Other worthwhile projects emerged as the study proceeded. For example, systematic studies were made of different methods of essay marking, of their reliability, and of procedures for assessing attitudes. Close analysis was made, too, of a variety of objective techniques for analysing the sentence structure in the essays written by the participating students. These matters will be discussed later in the text.

In considering the major purpose of the investigation, it is important to recognize that the stated justification for teaching grammar in the Oregon Curriculum is not specifically a utilitarian one—to improve language skills. Rather it is expected that those who study it will gain a greater understanding of a fundamental human activity. Any growth in language skills would be a by-product rather than the main goal. Thus an evaluation of the success of the language strand of the Oregon Curriculum cannot be achieved by an examination of its effects on writing skills alone. Nor can it be claimed that any assessment could be made of the validity of Chomsky's theories on the basis of this empirical study of the influence on children's language growth of one English curriculum which attempts to translate some of Chomsky's beliefs into classroom practice. That would be another issue entirely.

2

Lessons from Past Studies on the Role of Grammar

Research on Traditional Grammar

Writing in 1963, Richard Braddock claimed that all the research conducted on the effects of traditional grammar during the previous half-century, led to a strong and unqualified conclusion: 'the teaching of formal grammar has a negligible or—because it usually displaces some instruction and practice in actual composition—even a harmful effect on the improvement of writing'.[1]

It is easy to find support for such a gloomy assertion in the annals of research on English instruction. We could begin by inspecting the pioneering, if somewhat naive studies of correlations between knowledge of grammar and of composition, conducted in the first years of this century by Hoyt[2] and by Rapeer[3]. Such researchers found no more relationship between grammar and composition than existed between grammar and geography or arithmetic. We could examine, too, the small-scale experimental efforts of early amateur researchers, like Briggs[4] or Ash,[5] and draw similar conclusions. Short courses in formal grammar were shown to have no apparent influence on writing skills. And more recently we

1. R. Braddock et al., *Research in Written Composition* (Champaign, Illinois: NCTE, 1963).

2. F. S. Hoyt, 'The Place of Grammar in the Elementary Curriculum', in *Teachers College Record,* vol. 7, pp. 467–98, 1906.

3. L. W. Rapeer, 'The Problem of Formal Grammar in Elementary Education', in *Journal of Educational Psychology*, vol. 4, 125–37, 1913.

4. T. H. Briggs, 'Formal English Grammar as a Discipline', in *Teachers College Record*, vol. 14, pp. 1–93, 1913.

5. I. O. Ash, 'An Experimental Evaluation of the Stylistic Approach in Teaching Written Composition', in *Journal of Experimental Education*, vol. 4, pp. 54–62, 1935.

have the evidence of such elaborate and carefully controlled investigations as those of Harris[6] or Maize,[7] using large numbers of students and various criteria of composition growth. Once again, the experimenters could find no evidence that a formal study of English grammar produces any practical benefit for the participating students. In at least a dozen reported experiments, from primary school to university level, the differences in writing or language skills produced by instruction in grammar are repeatedly either negligible—or favour the non-grammar group.[8]

But the matter cannot be allowed to rest there. A closer examination of these investigations reveals at least three general weaknesses;

(1) the majority of the experiments did not extend beyond one term;

(2) most were evaluated with a limited range of objective tests, or a single essay; and

(3) the influence of the participating English teachers' attitudes and skills could not be separated from that of the course which the pupils were taught.

These are serious faults, which we must dwell on at this point.

The brevity of experimental studies of grammar cannot be ignored when we consider that a number of studies (for example, Macaulay,[9] Harris[10]) indicate that pupils actually master very little of the grammar they are taught in school. What has not been learned can surely not be expected to transfer. Indeed, a strict interpretation of Piaget's theory of mental development would lead us to suppose that formal abstractions, such as are learned in English grammar, are not readily acquired until children reach a mental age of 13 or 14 years, a level which a significant proportion of the population will never achieve. Therefore, we should be sceptical of any experiment which was not carried on for at least two years, and well into the pupils' high school course. In most investigations this has not been the case, chiefly, one suspects, because the researcher was bent on completing a graduate degree under the usual constraints and time pressures.

The second criticism, that of the paucity of criteria used to evaluate the effects of the grammar, may arise from the same pressures. Written language is a complex, multi-dimensional form of behaviour, notoriously slow in its development, inconstant in its quality, and extremely sensitive to the conditions under which it is elicited. Linguists like to emphasize the difference between a pupil's language *competence* and his *performance*, between his ability to compose or correct a sentence according to rule,

6. R. J. Harris, 'An Experimental Inquiry into the Functions and Value of Formal Grammar in the Teaching of English', PhD dissertation, University of London, 1962.

7. R. C. Maize, 'A Study of Two Methods of Teaching English Composition to Retarded Freshmen', PhD dissertation, Purdue University, 1952.

8. For a comprehensive summary of this research, see H. C. Meckel, 'Research on Teaching Composition and Literature', in *Handbook of Research on Teaching*, ed. N. L. Gage (Chicago: Rand McNally, 1963).

9. W. J. Macaulay, 'The Difficulty of Grammar', in *British Journal of Educational Psychology*, vol. 17, pp. 153–62, 1947.

10. R. J. Harris, *op. cit.*

and what he may actually write or utter in a given situation. In other words, an objective test of sentence structure, or sentence correction, although easy to prepare and validate, may reveal little about a pupil's habitual mode of writing, which is normally the quality that the English teacher aims to influence. The only really valid measure of composition skills is a composition exercise, and many of the grammar experiments cited have studiously avoided this criterion.

Those projects which have used essay writing as a criterion have frequently used only one such exercise. It might have been a narrative or descriptive essay, but it was seldom both, and it was usually confined to one topic, without choice. For those familiar with the problems of re-liability of essay marking and the low correlations found between different styles of essay, it is plain that a series of essays written on various topics and on different days, marked by several judges, would provide a more sensitive index of the impact of grammar tuition on writing skills, as Diederich explains.[11] Moreover, the subjective nature of the usual forms of assessment makes it important to identify objective indices of language structure which might be examined and counted, indices of sentence complexity, subordination and transformations, in addition to the more common assessments of correctness based on simple mechanics. Indeed, a cursory glance at the descriptions of previous studies shows that most ex-perimenters were preoccupied with counting mechanical errors, with very little emphasis on assessing the extent to which the students had increased the range and complexity of their sentence structures.

The third weakness of the experiments conducted on English grammar concerns the unknown influence of teacher characteristics on the outcome. Most studies have compared only two classes, taught sometimes by the same teacher, sometimes by two different teachers. In the latter case, there is no way of telling whether observed differences in achievement are due to the influence of the teacher or of the course; in the former case, we cannot be sure that the teacher's views on the value of grammar were not the critical factor in determining the result of the experiment. In all studies of this kind, a number of teachers should be used, so that the effects of teachers' attitudes and competence are minimized.

The single study which seems to rise above most of the criticisms cited above is that undertaken by Harris[12] in England, and the results certainly give adherents of traditional grammar teaching no cause for optimism. Harris compared the effects of instruction in formal grammar with those of a non-grammar course in general usage and problems of sentence structure. The grammar course was based on a traditional text-book; the non-grammar groups used no textbook, and studied common errors in composition, using inductive methods and patterned practice.

Two classes in each of five schools participated in the experiment, over a period of two years. It did not prove administratively feasible to match

11. P. B. Diederich, *Measuring Growth in English* (Champaign, Illinois: NCTE, 1974).

12. R. J. Harris, *op. cit.*

the pupils by ability in each group but, by good fortune, they proved to be nearly equivalent. In four of the five schools, one English teacher taught both grammar and non-grammar groups and, although this is no guarantee of partiality, the experimenter did vouch that 'all the teachers were willing to be convinced by the evidence'.

The measures used to evaluate the courses were a test of formal grammar and an essay, administered both before and after the experiment. The pre-test essay topic was 'A Day in the Country'; the post-test was 'A Day at the Seaside'. Rather than assess the essays subjectively, Harris made frequency counts of 11 objective criteria, which he had validated in a pilot project. These criteria included sentence length, number of common errors, subordinate clauses, total words, adjectival phrases, and the like.

As anticipated, the grammar group made much larger gains than the non-grammar group on the test of formal grammar. On the essay criteria, the results were inconclusive on an intermediate test given after one year. After two years, however, 11 of the possible 55 comparisons in the five schools favoured the non-grammar group, chiefly on the criteria of sentence complexity, and incidence of errors. On the other criteria, the differences were mostly insignificant.

Harris's study bears out, in the first place, the danger of drawing conclusions from short-term studies. The significant differences that he found took two years to appear. Furthermore, the study gives little encouragement to those who expect formal grammar instruction to improve children's writing. It is a pity that only one essay was used, and that the significant differences observed between the courses were all relatively small. The negative conclusion that Harris draws seems to require corroboration from other studies, designed along similar lines, with somewhat tighter controls.

In view of the apparent weaknesses of these investigations into the effects of grammar instruction, we must be wary of the pessimistic conclusions reached by Braddock and others who have reviewed the research to date. There may indeed be no evidence that traditional grammar has any appreciable effects on the improvement of writing skills. But we cannot assert, without fear of contradiction, that there *is* no effect. With properly matched teachers and pupils, and a well-taught course over a protracted period, a sensitive set of measurements may in fact reveal significant changes in writing style or structure which could be attributed to instruction in grammar.

In his extensive review of the subject, Meckel[13] agrees that 'there is no research evidence that grammar, as traditionally taught in the schools, has an appreciable effect on the improvement of writing skills', but is careful to add that 'there is no conclusive evidence, however, that grammar has no transfer value in developing composition skill'. The main reasons for Meckel's persistent open-mindedness seem to stem from two considerations:

13. H. C. Meckel, *op. cit.*

(1) The evidence that pupils in the research studies had actually learned very little grammar in the course of the experiments.

(2) No experiment has been conducted with children of above average intelligence, who were taught grammar to the point of mastery.

It seems then that the perfectly controlled experiment has yet to be designed, and so on the role of traditional grammar in children's composition skills the cautious researcher must perforce continue to be open-minded.

Meanwhile the traditional English teacher, seeking support for his continuing faith in the benefits of grammar, would seem unwise to justify it in terms of its utility. To hope for empirical support on the pragmatic usefulness of traditional grammar, is in the face of current evidence, a rather fond hope.

Research on Transformational Grammar

In the past 15 years, the role of traditional grammar in the English curriculum has been threatened from another quarter. The introduction and rapid spread of new linguistic grammars has reopened the same questions that researchers had asked about their traditional forerunner. Claims have been made that transformational grammar, in particular, is superior because it gets below the surface structure and relates the form and content of a sentence. Writers such as Bateman and Zidonis[14] and McGuire[15] see values in transformational grammar which should make it more meaningful and helpful for high school students, and many new textbooks and curricula in English have been designed on this assumption. Similar optimism has been expressed for other linguistic grammars.

What evidence do we have on the value of transformational grammar in the development of writing skills? Does a study of such grammar influence a student's sentence complexity, or correctness of expression? Or is its role also to be confined to that of an expected component of liberally-educated students, as 'a good thing to know'? And, if it has a role, what sacrifices might be made in the language growth of those who devote their time to it? These are questions on which educational research can be expected to throw some light.

In an early American study, Bateman and Zidonis[16] analysed the effects of a study of transformational-generative (TG) grammar on the writing of ninth grade students at a university laboratory school over a two-year period. Fifty students were randomly assigned to two classes, one of which had regular TG lessons. The teacher of the control group followed the 'regular' school English programme. Six pre-test and six post-test essays

14. D. R. Bateman and F. J. Zidonis, *The Effect of a Study of Grammar on the Writing of Ninth and Tenth Graders* (Champaign, Illinois: NCTE, 1966).
15. E. J. McGuire, 'Sentence Building and Transformational Grammar', in *English Journal* vol. 56, pp. 747–50, 1967.
16. D. R. Bateman and F. J. Zidonis, *op. cit.*

were written by both experimental and control classes. These essays were analysed meticulously for 'errors' and for structural complexity—the number of transformations per sentence. The results showed large and significantly superior gains for the experimental group in the proportion of sentences 'free of errors' (31.8 percent as against 3.5 percent), and a nearly significant advantage in the growth of sentence complexity. In reviewing this study, Mellon[17] points out that this difference in sentence complexity was in fact significant and the original authors unnecessarily cautious in their interpretation. Bateman and Zidonis concluded that their TG course did enable the students to improve their writing, and, with some qualification, that they had increased their ability 'to produce well-formed sentences of greater structural complexity'.

Several methodological weaknesses prevent us from accepting these conclusions, however. The grammar group was not only small (21 students) and atypical, but it was also brighter than the control group by an average of more than three IQ points. Furthermore, the significant improvements were, as the authors admit, confined to four students. No description is given of the programme pursued by the control group, so we are unable to determine what the TG grammar course was being compared with, and it appears that no control was exercised over the comparative skills and attitudes of the two teachers involved. The optimism of the authors may have been warranted, and their methods of composition analysis certainly represented an important step forward, but the evidence of this small experiment on the value of TG grammar is clearly insufficient to generalize from.

In a subsequent short-term study of eighth graders, Davis[18] studied the effects of instruction in grammar on four sentence structure variables, and compared the results with those shown by students studying traditional grammar. After a period of 14 weeks, the TG group showed small but significant increases in two of the four variables, predicate expansions and total number of clauses written, while the traditional group did not. This study is suggestive, but its brevity and limited controls still leave the question open.

Comparable studies have also been conducted on the value of instruction in structural grammar, mostly in America. One such investigation was carried out at university level by Johnson[19]. The design and experimental controls of this study make it worthy of attention as it involved 250 students who were allotted randomly into 12 classes, 6 to take a course in structural grammar, and 6 in traditional grammar. Each of the six participating teachers took a class in both programmes, and the experiment continued for three years. Evaluation was carried out using a variety of techniques including impromptu essays, tests of grammar, spelling,

17. J. C. Mellon, *Transformational Sentence-Combining* (Champaign, Illinois: NCTE, 1969).

18. M. W. Davis, 'A Comparative Analysis of Sentences written by Eighth Grade Students instructed in TG Grammar and Traditional Grammar', PhD dissertation, Boston University, 1967.

19. F. S. Johnson, 'Structural versus Non-Structural Teaching', in *College Composition and Communication*, vol. 11, p. 215, 1960.

vocabulary, scholastic aptitude, and academic record. On all criteria, however, the two groups showed a similar degree of improvement in the three-year period. At university level, it appeared that structural grammar, using regular training in oral drills and patterns, produced no significant advantage over traditional grammar.

More promising results were obtained at junior high school level by White,[20] in a one-year experiment in which he compared the effects of instruction in structural grammar with those obtained in traditional grammar and free reading courses. Using the STEP Writing Test, and comparing essays written both before and after the experiment, White concluded that the structural grammar group made significantly greater gains than either of the other two groups. The discrepancy between these two studies on structural grammars could well be accounted for by the age of the students involved. Those who have already passed through high school might have already acquired enough grammar for it to have its influence on writing—or alternatively the writing styles of these older students might have matured to the point where grammar instruction would be of less direct benefit.

Several other minor experiments of varying degrees of sophistication were conducted on structural or transformational grammars in the 1960s, but none produced any notable results until the substantial investigation undertaken by Mellon.[21] He set out to investigate the effects on the writing maturity of American seventh grade students of systematic training in sentence-combining, taught within the framework of a one-year course in transformational grammar. The 247 participating students came from schools in Massachusetts and were divided into 3 matched groups. The experimental group of 100 students studied specially prepared TG lessons for the first half-year, including exercises in which basic sentences were rewritten in their alternate forms. In the second half-year the students' grammar study focussed intensively on sentence-combining problems in which sets of kernel sentences were to be combined into more complex structures, with the aid of models and cues.

Sample problem:

Kernel sentences: (1) Officer Hermes ambled over towards the car.
                    (2) Officer Hermes only wanted a light for his pipe.
                    (3) He had flagged the car down out of the traffic lane.

Combined sentence: Officer Hermes, who only wanted a light for his pipe, ambled over toward the car, which he had flagged down out of the traffic lane.

With practice, the students were able to master successively more complex sentences, and apparently obtained much satisfaction in doing so.

The second group, also of 100 students, studied traditional grammar and usage exercises, while a third group of 47 students devoted their time

20. R. H. White, 'The Effect of Structural Linguistics on Improving English Composition', PhD dissertation, University of Arizona, 1965.

21. J. C. Mellon, *op. cit.*

to composition, usage exercises, and extra work in literature. No grammar was studied in this group. All the students wrote nine compositions on various topics in the first month of the school year, and another parallel set of nine at the end of the year. The effects of the three programmes were assessed by comparing changes in the number and kind of structures used by students in their essays.

The structural analysis used as a base was the T-unit rather than the complete sentence, since previous work by Hunt[22] had shown that the T-unit (defined as a main clause plus any subordinate clauses attached to it) provided a more sensitive index of syntactic maturity in school children. An analysis was made of the following 12 factors for each 100 T-units: T-unit length (words), ratio of subordination to coordination, noun clauses, noun phrases, relative clauses, relative phrases, relative words, embedded kernel sentences, clusters (of modifiers), mean cluster size embedding frequency, and the mean depth level of the most deeply, embedded sentences. On all 12 factors, Mellon found a significantly greater gain for the experimental group over the traditional grammar group. Comparison with Hunt's figures for norms of language growth indicated that for the TG group the rate of syntactic growth was twice that expected in the time period covered, clearly an important finding.

On the glacially-slow path towards maturity in syntactic structure, as indicated by developmental studies of the sentence structure of children and adults, the students who had been exposed to only five months of sentence-combining exercises in a TG context had made substantial growth. By contrast the traditional grammar and the non-grammar groups had made virtually no gains at all. The observed patterns of growth were similar for both sexes, all levels of ability, and each type of school. A small sample of essays was subsequently assessed for more orthodox qualitative differences between the three groups, but the results were inconclusive. It was claimed, however, that the style of the TG students had not been affected adversely by their unusual training.

Whether the impressive gains shown by the experimental group were artificial and temporary it is difficult to surmise. No follow-up studies were conducted to examine this assumption. But insofar as rapid progress was made by the pupils on a dimension of writing which is seldom affected by deliberate instruction, it is a finding which cannot be ignored. Mellon was careful to point out that we cannot conclude that the grammar itself was the critical factor. In his view, which seems highly plausible, it was the sentence-combining exercises which effected the improvement. The experimental design of the study was exemplary in many respects, but on this particular issue there remains some doubt. From this experiment we can only conclude that the kinds of construction exercise practised by the students in a TG context brought about important developments in sentence structure, without any apparent undesirable side-effects in other aspects of their writing style.

22. K. W. Hunt, *Grammatical Structures Written at Three Grade Levels* (Champaign, Illinois: NCTE, 1965).

Since Mellon's study, further experiments by Fry[23] and by Thompson and Middleton[24] have shown that the influence of instruction in transformational grammar on the writing style of high school students is indeed very slight. If the evidence of these studies is adequate, then Mellon's case is clearly supported, that it was the sentence-combining exercises rather than the transformational grammar per se that was crucial. However, in both these cases the instruction in transformational grammar was only one semester in length, scarcely enough to produce definite results.

A subsequent study of O'Hare[25] showed that seventh grade pupils taught sentence-combining skills over a period of eight months did show significant improvements in their syntactic maturity, when compared with a control group taking no such programme. Furthermore, their essay writing was judged superior in general quality by a panel of eight experienced English teachers. Since the experimental exercises were prepared in such a way that they did not depend on the students' prior knowledge of grammar, traditional or transformational, O'Hare concluded that it was, in fact, the sentence-combining practice that achieved the positive results. While this study does confirm much of Mellon's work, and points to a promising direction for further study, it still leaves unanswered the question of the role of grammar itself in bringing about changes in children's writing growth.

Conclusion

When the current experiment was undertaken, the best evidence available suggested that there could well be practical value in transformational grammar, quite apart from the liberal reasons for teaching it. The studies of Bateman and Zidonis, Davis, and Mellon seemed to point in this direction, although all had to be seriously qualified, the first two for their small scale, the latter for its unusual curricular aims and content. The question then was still undecided, leaving linguists and teachers to persist in their contrary views. New high school texts in grammar have continued to appear, and English teachers have continued to stress grammar in their lessons.

The present authors, believing the subject to be accessible to empirical study, and concerned that the crucial experiment had not yet been conducted, spent much time reviewing the research reported above. We learnt much from their mistakes, but even more from their methods of analysis and their sanguine interpretations. It gradually became clear that if the utility value of transformational grammar in affecting composition was to be tested, then an experiment was needed in which the grammar

23. J. Fry, 'The Effects of Transformational Grammar upon the Writing Performance of Students of Low Socio-Economic Background', PhD dissertation, Memphis State University, 1971.

24. C. L. Thompson and M. H. Middleton, 'Transformational Grammar and Inductive Teaching as Determinants of Structurally Complex Writing', in *California Journal of Educational Research*, No. 24, pp. 28–41, 1973.

25. F. O'Hare, *Sentence Combining; Improving Student Writing without Formal Grammar Instruction*, (Champaign, Illinois: NCTE, 1973).

was taught (to the point of mastery), over a period of two or three years at least. Over this period students' writing should be assessed for both structural and qualitative criteria, and, in order to check on side effects, assessments should be made of other language skills. The students should be carefully matched for ability, and, to control for the unpredictable effects of the teachers' attitudes and competence, several teachers should be used, preferably in a situation where each taught the grammar and non-grammar groups. Of the many studies reported in the extensive literature on the effects of grammar instruction, it seemed that none had followed these guidelines sufficiently well to reach firm conclusions.

3

Design of the Research Project

Our investigation was conducted entirely in one large coeducational high school, located on the outskirts of Auckland city. Within this school, 250 pupils of average ability were taught, observed and regularly assessed for a period of three years, from the beginning of their third form year, in February 1970, to the latter part of their fifth form year, in November 1972.[1] A follow-up test was subsequently given in November 1973.

It was felt that a three-year longitudinal study of a group of typical high school students would provide more satisfactory results than a shorter term study of a larger number of pupils from several schools. Restricting the study to one school facilitated communication between teachers, increased the likelihood of standardization of teaching and testing procedures, and generally ensured greater control in the experiment. The decision to continue the study for three years obviated the criticism that it would be too short a period for any effects on the students' writing to become apparent. The common limitation of earlier experiments, that the attitudes and skills of the participating English teachers could have an undue influence on the results, was circumvented somewhat by using three teachers of diverse backgrounds and personality, and by ensuring that, as far as circumstances permitted, each course was taught by each teacher to each class, at some stage in the three years of the project. Thus, the influence of each course could be distinguished from the influence of each teacher, and their relative effects and interactions observed by statistical procedures.

The pupils participating in the study were chosen in such a way that extremes of ability were deliberately excluded. A more homogeneous sample makes it easier to identify systematic differences between teaching programmes. Thus, one bright and three slow-learning classes of pupils

1. Pupils between the ages of about 12–16.

from the total third form intake of 380 pupils were omitted, leaving eight classes of near-average ability. It was fortunate that the school organization already allowed for such grouping to take place.

Reading test scores from the Progressive Achievement Test series[2] showed the 250 pupils to be average in reading comprehension and vocabulary skills, while the distribution of fathers' occupations indicated a fair cross-section of a New Zealand urban community (see Tables 3.1 and 3.2). There were equal numbers of boys and girls in the experimental groups, and the proportion of Polynesians was not unusual (16 percent) for the third form of an Auckland suburban school. Subsequently, it was found that the overall pass rate in the School Certificate Examination of those remaining in the group after 3 years was 52 percent, which compares with the national pass rate of 50 percent.

Table 3.1

Means and Standard Deviations of Sample on PAT Reading Tests, Form B

	PAT Reading Comprehension		PAT Vocabulary	
	M	SD	M	SD
Sample	21.8	7.2	42.3	9.8
NZ Norms	23.1	9.8	41.4	13.1

Table 3.2

Percentage of Sample whose Fathers were Classified in each Category of NZCER Occupational Scale[3]

Level	1	2	3	4	5	6	Total
% in sample	9	8	16	34	25	8	100
% in NZ urban areas	7	11	23	29	21	9	100

Classification of Pupils

In 1970, the first year of the project, the total third form intake of pupils at the school consisted of 380 pupils grouped into 12 classes. The children were classified on the basis of general verbal ability into three levels: one

2. W. B. Elley and N. A. Reid, *Progressive Achievement Tests of Reading* (Wellington: NZCER, 1969).
3. W. B. Elley and J. C. Irving, 'Revised Socio-Economic Index for New Zealand', in *New Zealand Journal of Educational Studies*, vol. 11, no. 1, May 1976.

bright class, eight average classes, and three slow-learning groups. Specifically, the information used to make these classifications was obtained from the General Ability Test (GAT), prepared by G. L. Arvidson,[4] from Otis IQ results and from the assessments made by contributing schools.

The eight classes of average pupils were carefully matched to ensure that they were equivalent in terms of size, general ability, reading comprehension, reading vocabulary, English language usage, and with the proportions of children from each sex, ethnic group, contributing school and subject options. Table 3.3 sets out the relevant means and standard deviations on all the matching tests for each of the eight classes at the beginning of the experiment.

Table 3.3

Means and Standard Deviations on Tests of General Ability and Language for all Classes

Class	Course	N	GAT M	GAT SD	Reading Comprehension M	Reading Comprehension SD	Vocabulary M	Vocabulary SD	English Language M	English Language SD
M_1	TG	31	13.5	3.7	21.5	6.5	41.6	9.8	22.4	5.0
M_2	TG	31	13.3	3.6	21.2	7.3	43.9	9.7	24.4	4.2
M_3	RW	31	13.6	3.4	21.6	6.5	41.7	9.5	22.4	3.6
M_4	RW	31	13.3	3.7	21.9	7.1	41.8	10.0	24.5	4.5
M_5	TG	31	13.4	3.2	21.8	8.3	42.7	10.7	23.6	4.6
M_6	LLE	31	13.4	3.4	21.2	6.1	41.4	9.5	24.1	5.1
M_7	RW	31	13.3	3.4	22.3	7.6	44.6	9.3	23.7	5.6
M_8	LLE	31	13.2	3.5	21.9	7.5	41.2	9.8	24.2	3.6

The three courses studied by the pupils in the project are described briefly below. A fuller description is contained in Chapter 4.

(1) The Transformational Grammar (TG) course included the grammar, rhetoric and literature 'strands' of the Oregon English Curriculum.

(2) The Reading-Writing (RW) course included the rhetoric and literature strands of the Oregon Curriculum, but substituted extra reading and creative writing for the Transformational Grammar strand.

(3) The *Let's Learn English* (LLE) course was included to be typical of those found in New Zealand secondary schools at the time of the project. The three textbooks which provided most of the work in composition, comprehension and 'functional' grammar are named *Let's Learn English*, 3, 4, and 5, and were written by P. R. Smart, a

---

4. G. L. Arvidson, *General Ability Test*. See 'The Hutt Valley Classification Scheme', unpublished document (Wellington: Victoria University of Wellington, 1958).

New Zealand teacher of English. Other prose readers and poetry anthologies were also used. The textbooks were seen as source books rather than as an integrated course in themselves.

Originally it was intended to compare only the TG and RW programmes, using six classes. As two more average classes were available, however, it was decided to broaden the scope of the project by evaluating the whole of the Oregon Curriculum in relation to a typical New Zealand course.

Thus, the design allowed for three classes to study the TG programme, three to follow the RW course, and the remaining two to take the LLE course. Three teachers were involved in the experiment throughout the three years. Each took a TG class and an RW class in each year, and two of the three taught an LLE class. The classes and teachers were assigned at random: the classes followed the same programme throughout, but the teachers changed classes each year. In the third year, the constraints of timetabling and subject choice made it necessary to introduce two additional teachers to take the two LLE classes.

Each of the three main teachers involved in the project was a fully qualified English teacher; two had a Masters degree and one a BA (Hons). At the beginning of the investigation the two male teachers had taught for 14 and 6 years respectively, the female teacher for 1 year. Each volunteered to participate in the project for the three-year period because of a genuine interest in the outcomes. No detectable bias was apparent in their approach to their teaching of any of the courses. The two additional teachers who took the LLE classes in the fifth form year were also fully qualified, experienced teachers, who willingly agreed to participate with an open mind as to the outcomes.

The design of the experiment, showing the organization of pupils, teachers and courses, is illustrated in tabular form below. To illustrate the interpretation of this table an example may be helpful. Class M_1 was taught the TG course, by Teacher A in Form 3, Teacher B in Form 4, and Teacher C in Form 5. At the beginning of the experiment in February 1970, the class contained 31 pupils. This number had dropped to 29 by November 1970, and to 20 by November 1972.

Some mention should be made of the pupils who left or arrived during the course of the project. New arrivals were included if they entered the school within the first four months of the first year. To identify any possible bias in the results, due to changes caused as pupils left or entered the various classes, the test scores on which the groups were initially matched were recalculated for the particular samples of pupils remaining at each evaluation point in the project.

As Table 3.4 shows, there was a considerable decline in numbers of pupils over the three years. Total numbers actually dropped from 248 in February 1970 to 166 in November 1972. Nevertheless, the mean scores of the three groups on the relevant matching variables remained almost identical to one another. Thus the three programmes were taught to

Table 3.4
Organization of Pupils, Teachers and Courses, 1970–72

Classes	Courses	Teachers F3	F4	F5	N in Feb 1970	N in Nov 1970	N in Nov 1971	N in Nov 1972
M_1	TG	A	B	C	31	29	22	20
M_2	TG	C	A	B	31	31	25	20
M_5	TG	B	C	A	31	31	24	22
M_3	RW	C	A	B	31	31	26	22
M_4	RW	A	B	C	31	28	22	18
M_7	RW	B	C	A	31	28	27	22
M_6	LLE	C	A	D	31	31	24	20
M_8	LLE	A	C	E	31	30	25	22

groups which could be regarded as very similar in their language achievement and aptitude throughout Form 3, Form 4 and Form 5. Tables 3.5 and 3.6 show the means of the three groups on the matching tests for the pupils who remained in the experiment in Forms 4 and 5 respectively.

Table 3.5
Matching Test Means for Sample at End of Form 4 Year

Course	GAT	Reading Comprehension	Reading Vocabulary	English Language
TG	13.96	23.09	44.40	24.12
RW	14.06	22.45	44.00	24.24
LLE	14.00	22.67	43.13	24.86

Table 3.6
Matching Test Means for Sample at End of Form 5 Year

Course	GAT	Reading Comprehension	Reading Vocabulary	English Language
TG	14.20	23.87	45.74	24.17
RW	14.35	23.55	45.78	25.00
LLE	14.32	22.98	43.68	24.68

C

4

The Oregon Curriculum in English

This chapter provides a description of the Oregon English Curriculum,[1] a text book course in English, which formed the basis for work done by two of the research groups. As this is a relatively new course, unfamiliar to many teachers of English, its main features will be described at some length. Chapter 5 offers a description, in greater detail, of the courses of work actually undertaken by all three research groups, giving specific information on the teaching procedures, timetabling and related topics.

General Aims and Structure of the Curriculum

In September 1961 the United States Office of Education founded 'Project English'. Seven 'Curriculum Study Centres' were set up throughout the United States to develop and test experimental English curricula. The Oregon Curriculum, now published as a regular textbook series, has its origin in one of these study centres.

One important characteristic of the Curriculum is the unusually simple and clear focus of its aims, in contrast to the array of nebulous objectives commonly set for English courses. All teaching activities are readily seen to be related to the central core of each of the three 'strands' of the curriculum, thus giving it clear and consistent unity of purpose.

The three aims, broadly stated, are first, to increase the students' command of the basic skills of communication; secondly, to foster insight and enjoyment in the reading of a wide variety of literature; and, finally, to interest students in their language, its structure, and how it works. The three strands of the Curriculum, Rhetoric, Literature and Language, are designed around these three primary aims.

1. A. R. Kitzhaber, ed., *The Oregon Curriculum: A Sequential Program in English* (New York: Holt, Rinehart and Winston, 1968).

A second feature of the Oregon Curriculum is the determination of the authors to remain true to the principles of the subject as revealed by the most up-to-date thought and research of leading scholars. Although these underlying concepts are introduced simply, using material which is carefully selected to appeal to young people, they are consistent with our best knowledge about the subject. Thus, they preserve its integrity.

Another important characteristic of the Curriculum is its sequential, cumulative nature. It is based on the principle enunciated by J. S. Bruner in *The Process of Education.*[2] He suggested that at the heart of any discipline is a set of basic concepts which can be taught to young people in an elementary but intellectually honest way; these concepts can subsequently be returned to and elaborated at a more advanced level.

As Kitzhaber, the General Editor says: 'We have selected a few of the central organizing principles of literature or rhetoric or grammar, as the case may be, those principles which confer structure and identity on an otherwise amorphous body of data, and we have presented these principles through simple applications in the early years and more complex and sophisticated applications as the child grows older. Then the curriculum returns again and again to the same matters in a widening spiral, reinforcing the students' understanding of those central concepts that lead not merely to the possession of a body of facts but to an understanding of their significance.'[3]

Another distinctive feature is that the Oregon Curriculum is designed for learning to be *inductive* as well as cumulative and sequential. Wherever possible, material is presented in such a way that students are led for the most part to discover concepts and derive conclusions for themselves.

(1)   *The Rhetoric Strand*

The objective of the Rhetoric Strand is to develop effective communication. The term *rhetoric* was chosen because it implies not only a form of self-expression, but composition which is deliberate, thoughtful and designed to have a particular effect on an audience. Reading, writing, speaking, and listening are not dominated by standards of correctness—this is an adjunct only. Usage, spelling, punctuation and writing quality are considered from the point of view of *effectiveness*, or achievement of purpose, rather than any absolute standard of correctness.

Underlying the whole strand, then, is the notion of *purpose*. An awareness of purpose determines the shape of every assignment. The pupil is repeatedly brought face to face with the necessity to consider the needs of his audience.

The assumption is made, too, that there is an underlying *structure* in composition. This structure is teachable, first simply, then in increasingly sophisticated applications, after the manner of Bruner's notion of the spiral.

2. J. S. Bruner, *The Process of Education* (Cambridge: Harvard University Press, 1962).
3. A. R. Kitzhaber, *op. cit.*

To achieve one's purpose effectively requires control of three elements, basic to the structure of composition. *Substance* is concerned with facts and ideas which form the raw content for the act of communication; *structure* refers to the organization and development of the substance chosen; *style* is concerned with the use of words and sentences in such a way that the desired rhetorical purpose will be achieved.

Specific topics studied in the course included writing to inform, explain, and persuade; organization; adapting writing to a particular audience; creating humour, suspense, drama, dialogue, and so on. All such topics are related to the basic concerns of substance, structure and style.

(2)   *The Literature Strand*

The literature strand of the Oregon Curriculum has been planned with care and discrimination. Its aims are primarily educative and humane: literature is studied for its own sake rather than for some external or utilitarian purpose. It is therefore quite different from studies of literature based upon a single theme or which illustrate an historical trend. In such courses the nature of the work of art often becomes less important than one aspect of it, its subject. The contents of the Oregon Curriculum are selected in such a way as to enable students to enjoy them for their own sake. It is intended also to help students discover key concepts in literature, so that their ability to understand and enjoy the works of literature and other media which they meet outside the curriculum is increased. Again the spiral notion is adopted to achieve the underlying aims of this strand. The basic concepts of *subject, form,* and *point of view* are isolated, developed in depth, and returned to at successively more advanced levels in later stages of the course.

Any work of literature is, of course, an integral whole, and any dissection of it is to some extent artificial. Nevertheless, the authors of this curriculum believe that students can be helped towards a fuller enjoyment of literature by developing an awareness of these three fundamental concepts, any one of which can provide a starting point for a deeper study of the whole work.

The concept of *subject* is shown to have two aspects: *concrete* and *abstract.* The concrete subject refers to the facts and events of the selections; the abstract subject refers to the generalizations invited by the work, the ideas and attitudes stimulated in the reader's mind. This abstract subject is often referred to as the *theme*; in the Oregon Curriculum the word *theme* is used to apply not to particular ideas but to the more general area of concern of the literary work, such as the struggle of man against nature, or a study of family relationships.

In its treatment of the *form* of a literary selection, the Oregon Curriculum directs the student to examine the verbal and artistic structure of ideas, not only within each work, but also in comparison with other literature of the same genre. Some insight into the form of the work is believed to heighten the reader's enjoyment of it.

The technical meaning of *point of view* is concerned with the angle of narration, either first or third person, and their many related variations. In addition, the point of view refers to the attitudes involved in the work, whether held by the athor, the characters, or the reader.

These three basic concepts—subject, form, and point of view—are introduced and developed in the third form course (Literature I and II), but by the fifth form level, greater emphasis is placed on the unity of the work, and there is less isolation of the three concepts. Like the other strands, the literature course is designed to be taught inductively. Each successive work is chosen to cater for student interest, and is presented in such a way that it will reinforce concepts already learned and enable the student to enlarge his understanding and see for himelf new applications of the ideas developed earlier. The Teacher's Guide, which accompanies each volume, emphasizes that the analysis should not be carried to the point where it interferes with the enjoyment of the work.

Each literature book contains the year's work under one cover. In each book there are 20 to 30 poems, 6 or 7 short stories, and several selections in non-fiction and drama. The year's work is brought together in the study of a novel at the end, and an anthology of additional selections for extension and enrichment follows each section. The books are visually most attractive, being generously illustrated with multi-coloured pictures. The selections for the third form text include 14 narrative poems, 20 lyric poems, 6 autobiographical extracts, 7 travel and adventure extracts, 9 anthologies, 2 plays and a novel. The material in later texts covers a similarly wide range.

The emphasis in the concepts studied varies from year to year. For example, in Literature IV, studied in the fifth form, the attitudinal point of view is stressed, so that the non-fiction section consists largely of satirical essays. On the other hand, in Literature II, the corresponding section includes more first person narration of personal experience and adventure.

(3) *The Language Strand*

The central purpose of the language strand is seen in the development of a transformational grammar of English. The text for each year also includes chapters on such aspects of language as the origins of English, human and animal language, and writing systems.

TRANSFORMATIONAL GRAMMAR[4]

Transformational grammar assumes that in any sentence, there are two kinds of structure—*deep structure* and *surface structure*. Sentences actually spoken or heard are examples of surface structure, but a native speaker may understand elements which do not appear in that surface structure. Consider for example, the sentence *Put down your pen*. A native speaker

---

4. This description is derived from the Introduction to the Teacher's Guide to the language strand of the Oregon Curriculum, to which readers who want a fuller statement are referred.

understands another element that does not appear in that sentence, namely the element *you*. He knows that the sentence means the same as *You put down your pen*. The *you* exists in the deep structure but does not appear in the surface structure. Because the two sentences mean the same thing, we say that they have the same deep structure. In other words, the deep structure describes what we understand by the sentence.

Consider another example. Native speakers of English will know that *The traveller opens the suitcase* and *The suitcase is opened by the traveller* mean the same thing. What the traveller does and what happens to the suitcase are the same in both sentences. Thus, because we understand the same thing from both sentences we say that they have the same deep structure; but what we hear or read is different in each sentence, so we say that they have different surface structures.

In some sentences the deep structure is obvious—there is no essential difference between the surface structure and the deep structure; no major changes have been made to the deep structure in producing the surface structure. Such sentences can be called basic sentences. On the other hand it is often the case that because many changes have been made—by deletion, rearrangement of elements, and so on—the surface structure appears to bear little relation to the deep structure. Even so, native speakers know intuitively the relationship of the parts of the deep structure. Transformational grammar sets out to describe the deep and surface structures of sentences and the transformations that are made in producing the surface structure. It explains in the form of a number of rules the apparently instinctive knowledge possessed by native speakers of language.

Now the number of rules which need to be set out is limited. Obviously a native speaker does not need a different rule for each sentence he utters. Yet the number of different sentences which can be produced by a native speaker is unlimited because he can use the limited set of rules he knows in order to combine sentence parts in a great variety of ways. This principle is known as *recursiveness*. The internalized knowledge the speaker has of the set of rules he uses to produce sentences is referred to as his *linguistic competence*.

THE RULES

The transformational grammarian attempts to describe the set of rules which a native speaker naturally uses. The rules are of two kinds: *phrase structure* rules and *transformation* rules.

Phrase structure rules identify the parts of basic sentences and show how they are related in the deep structure. Here are examples of some of these rules, which are then used to make a partial analysis of the deep structure of a simple sentence.

$$S \rightarrow NP + VP$$

This rule states that a sentence (S) consists of ($\rightarrow$) a noun phrase (NP) and a verb phrase (VP).

NP→$\begin{Bmatrix} DP+N \\ Pro \end{Bmatrix}$

The brace ({ }) indicates an *either or* element, so that this rule states that a noun phrase (NP) consists of (→) *either* a determiner phrase (DP) and a noun (N), *or* a pronoun (Pro).

VP→Aux+MVP

A verb phrase (VP) consists of (→) an Auxiliary Verb Phrase (Aux) and a Main Verb Phrase (MVP).

Aux→Tns . . .

An Auxiliary Verb Phrase (Aux) consists of Tense (Tns). Other optional elements are omitted here for the sake of simplicity.

MVP→V+(NP) . . .

The parentheses show that an element is optional. This rule states that a Main Verb Phrase (MVP) consists of a verb (V) and can include a Noun Phrase, as well as other optional elements not shown here.

These phrase structure rules show what parts a sentence can consist of, and what the components and relationships of those parts are. These relationships can also be conveyed diagrammatically. Consider, for example, the simple sentence:

The boys enjoyed the game.

The parts and their relationships as described by the above selection of rules, can be demonstrated like this:

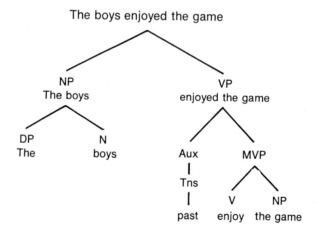

While phrase structure rules describe the parts of basic sentences and their relationships in the deep structure, other rules are needed to show the changes that occur as the surface structure is produced. These are transformation rules. For example; *can you drive* and *you can drive*

appear to be related; they are derived from the same deep structure. *The baby ripped my shirt* and *My shirt was ripped by the baby* are related; they have the same deep structure. Transformational rules show how the relationship of the parts in the deep structure was changed, so that two different surface structures were produced.

It is worth noting that it is not the intention of the Oregon Curriculum to present a complete grammar in English. The intention is to 'present some of the significant aspects of English grammar, and to help students see how they can discover facts about their language and how they use it'.

5

Details of Content and Teaching Procedures

As described previously, three different English courses were taught to three different groups of pupils for the three years of the project. The TG group studied the whole of the Oregon Curriculum. The RW group studied the Literature and Rhetoric Strands only, with additional periods of reading and writing to replace the language strand. The LLE groups used the *Let's Learn English* series by P. R. Smart as the basic text, with supplementary literature supplied from the resources of the school. All three groups had the same number and distribution of English periods throughout the week; a total of six periods—four in the morning and two in the afternoon. All groups had two English periods on the same day, Tuesday.

The three teachers involved had six periods throughout the week set aside for the general planning of the project. This time was used for the following activities: discussing and planning work to be covered, ensuring that methods of teaching were parallel, making up assignments and short tests for classroom use, moderating the marking of written assignments so that a uniform method and standard was maintained, reviewing and evaluating lessons taken, making suggestions for future lessons, and constructing major tests for the evaluation of students at the end of each year.

The TG Course

This course consisted of all three strands of the Oregon Curriculum, language (including grammar), rhetoric, and literature.

(a) *Language*

Form 3. The TG group began their study of the language strand in the second week of their first term in Form 3. Because the Oregon Curriculum is designed to commence in the New Zealand equivalent of Form 2, students could not begin work in the book designed for their age level, Language II, without first becoming familiar with the phrase structure rules of basic sentences, as outlined in Language I. Fortunately there was available a Self-Instructional Handbook accompanying the Oregon Curriculum, intended to acquaint new arrivals in a school with language work they have missed. This programmed material was adapted for the use of Form 3 class groups with the aid of overhead projector transparencies and cyclostyled work-books. The first six weeks of work in this strand were occupied with this introductory material from Language I. Its main purpose was to introduce students to phrase structure rules. This was accomplished by showing them how they use internalized rules whenever they produce sentences, and that grammar is a description of these rules. The students were familiarized with elements in the deep structure of sentences and with the relationships between them.

By the end of April, all three classes understood the basic phrase structure rules sufficiently well to move on to Language II. Here the main concepts were reinforced and students went on in their study of transformation rules to discover that only a relatively small number of rules are needed to produce an infinite number of sentences. They learned, for instance, that basic sentences can be combined to produce longer, more complicated sentences by coordination, as in *I work quickly and my brother works slowly.*

Another combination studied was that of *subordination*, in which one basic sentence is embedded within another. This type of embedding discussed in Language II concerned sentences which were embedded in noun phrases to produce noun modifiers such as:

the hat *that I wore*;
the *horrible* dinner;
the man *in the car*;
Michael's girlfriend.

Form 4. Students began work in Language III with a review chapter, taught by the teacher of the previous year. In the major part of the year's work the possibility of producing an infinite number of sentences by applying a limited number of rules was again illustrated, this time by concentrating on the changes which can occur to a single basic sentence to produce different surface structures. This meant a discussion of questions, negative sentences and passive sentences.

Form 5. In the first five chapters in Language IV there was a thorough revision of earlier work. New transformations in Chapters 6 and 7 built on rules describing embedded sentences which students had first encountered in Form Three. Examples of these more complex transformations are those which produce participle modifiers such as 'the *pleasing* suggestion', and 'the *frightened* boy'. Students then went on to examine the difference between restrictive and non-restrictive modifiers.

Because of the preparation time required for the School Certificate Examination in Form 5, it was not possible to complete the work in Language IV; students stopped at Chapter 7.

With the exception of parts of the introductory programmed material outlining the phrase structure rules, work in the language strand of the Oregon Curriculum has been so arranged that the students learn the rules inductively. Each chapter typically begins by reminding students of those aspects of grammar that they have already encountered, and which will be necessary for the discovery of a new feature. Sentences are then presented which differ from those previously seen, and pupils are asked to apply their existing knowledge to discover new rules. The class usually worked through several examples as each process unfolded. Some examples were done orally, some were worked by teacher or students on the blackboard, some were written individually by students. Often more topical sentences replaced textbook examples. Occasionally, grammar exercises were set for homework, not to introduce new material but to reinforce class work. Such exercises were normally given, however, only to enable classes to keep up to the required timetable.

Certain chapters in the language strand are not devoted to Transformational Grammar. These examine such issues as writing systems, the history of the language, and animal communication. As in the grammar section, the teaching emphasis was predominantly inductive. In Forms 3 and 4, from 12 to 15 periods were spent each year on these chapters. In Form 5 these sections were necessarily omitted. Work on the language strand was spread evenly throughout the year. For the proportions of time spent on the language strand in each year, see Table 5.1 at the end of this chapter.

ASSESSMENT OF TRANSFORMATIONAL GRAMMAR

In October of the third year of the project, and before the final testing programme, the three classes in the TG group spent a short time in revision of certain parts of the grammar course. They were then given certain sentences and asked to state the deep structure, or to draw branching diagrams, and write the transformations which had occurred. As 94 percent of the group were largely correct in their description of most sentences, it could be concluded that most students had achieved the aims of this section of the course. A more detailed analysis of results is given in Appendix 2.

(b) *Literature*

Each literature book of the Oregon Curriculum contains a preview section, which introduces the main area of concern for that year in a simple outline, illustrated with prose extracts, a short story and a poem. In addition, at the beginning of the first year, the students were issued with a general introduction to literature in the Oregon Curriculum, culled from Book I, consisting of a simple explanation of the basic concepts of *concrete* and *abstract subjects, form* and *point of view*, followed by illustrative poems, a short story and a fable, all with accompanying discussion questions. This material was given to classes before they had been issued with textbooks, or had started their normal timetable. Approximately six periods were spent on this introductory material.

The classes were then issued with the textbook, Literature II. They proceeded to work through the Preview material and the subsequent parts in sequence. In general the literature extracts were read aloud and discussed in class, with the teacher taking the major role. Parts of the longer works were read silently in class, or, in some cases, assigned for home-study after initial class discussion. Although the questions for discussion follow the selections in the textbook, the points raised in them were often discussed in the course of reading the selections. Occasionally, two or three questions were set for written homework, as were a few of the suggestions for composition and further activities.

Some class time was also spent on a study of the vocabulary and contextual meanings of the selection. However, most of the follow-up work in literature consisted of oral discussion. Any written work, such as that arising from the suggestions for composition, usually came at the end of a large section of work (for example, Narrative Poetry or the Short Story). It thus served to round off and consolidate the material covered in class, through the pupils' own writing. For example, after reading an extract from *The Red Pony*, pupils would be asked to find descriptions of concrete objects, to identify and reread passages of dialogue which 'reveal important things about the people in the story', and to find illustrations of sense imagery. Suggestions for composition would include the writing of a short original dialogue in a given situation, and of paragraphs which described minor characters in the story.

In the third form year, the study of drama in literature coincided with the chapter on drama in the Rhetoric strand. It was thus possible to integrate creative drama with a study of drama as literature. Pressure of time made it necessary to neglect many sections on word study and suggestions for composition. This time constraint, together with the apparent needs and ability levels of the pupils, led to the omission of the play by Shaw and the replacement of the novel *Separate Peace* in Literature IV with *Animal Farm*. The latter novel is suggested as extra reading for the course, and material for its study is provided in the Teacher's Guide.

Some time was also spent before the October (1972) school examinations in giving classes some experience in preparing for literature questions in the School Certificate Examination. This was considered important as the pupils in the project had had no third or fourth form examinations in which to gain this kind of experience.

(c) *Rhetoric*

In this strand, students began in February 1970 with a study of the Review, the first chapter of Rhetoric II. This gave an adequate introduction to the concepts underlying rhetoric and particularly to the concepts of *substance*, which was the main focus of Rhetoric I. At this stage, substance was concerned chiefly with the pupil's personal world of experience and fact.

The teaching moved systematically through the chapters of this strand at each class level. The third form work in rhetoric was built upon the fundamental concept of *purpose*. Students were made aware of the importance of purpose as it controls and shapes all communication; they undertook activities in speaking and writing organized around three of the basic purposes for communicating: to inform, to entertain, and to persuade. In Form 4, major attention shifted to *structure*; organizational patterns in sentences, paragraphs and longer compositions occupied the major part of the year's work. The emphasis in the fifth form returned to substance, the concept with which the course began. At this level, however, it was widened to include not just the writer's personal world, but also the world of abstract ideas, as the students came to grips with semantics and patterns of logical thinking.

New topics were usually initiated with the reading and discussion of the first extracts in a chapter; this helped the students to discover the main aim. Early extracts showed the idea in its simplest form, and each succeeding extract enabled classes to enlarge and elaborate on it. Discussion questions and some of the simpler exercises were dealt with orally, while more complex exercises were written. These activities were all planned to lead the students systematically towards the major goals of the strand.

ROUTINES FOR MARKING IN THE RHETORIC STRAND

It was considered important to introduce a consistent method of evaluating students' regular writing assignments. Therefore, early in the first year of the project, procedures were evolved for evaluating writing assignments according to the way each pupil had fulfilled the purpose of that chapter. No numerical rating was written on the pupil's work, but, for the purpose of the school's ten-weekly assessment system, a mark out of 10 was entered in the markbooks. On the pupils' written assignments, in place of a mark, the following general comments were written:

(a) Identification of some point on which they had done well and deserved credit.

(b) A verbal comment stating how well their assignment had achieved the purpose set.

(c) A specific suggestion for improving their achievement in the main teaching aim.

(d) A specific suggestion for improving the most obvious or serious mechanical fault of the assignment.

Where necessary, corrective exercises were set from the Usage section of the Rhetoric books. Generally, this practice saved class-time which would otherwise have been spent in reaching a point of usage needed by one or two pupils only. For example, in an assignment asking pupils to write to a relative, persuading them to lend their empty section for a Guy Fawkes bonfire, the teacher's comment might read:

> This is a very persuasive piece of writing, as you have used the 'you–viewpoint' well. More details about your party might reassure your uncle. Be careful with run-on sentences. The lines marked* have two sentences written as one. Divide them into two and check punctuation.

Pupils were asked to check their own and often their classmates' work four times, under each of the four following headings:

> *Substance*: Is the material chosen suitable for the purpose? For the audience? Are there supporting details? Are these effective? Are the *best* ideas included?
>
> *Structure*: How are the ideas put together? Are the paragraphs well organized? Is there an introduction? A conclusion?
>
> *Style*: Is there variety in choice of words? In sentence construction? In sentence length? Is the style appropriate to audience? To purpose?
>
> *Mechanics*: Does every sentence make sense? Is the spelling correct? Is every sentence punctuated clearly?

After a few months in the first year of the project, the marking system was amended to incorporate these four headings. Instead of a mark out of 10, a mark on a 1–4 scale, under each of the four categories, was recorded in the teachers' markbooks. No marks were recorded on the pupils' work.

The RW Course

The RW groups studied the same programmes in Literature and Rhetoric as those studied by the three classes following the TG Course. In place of the Transformational Grammar, however, the RW classes spent an average of two periods each week on extra reading and writing. The relevant details are outlined below.

(a) *Reading*

Approximately 40 percent of the reading and writing periods were spent in 'free' reading, either in the library or in English classrooms. Students were given considerable freedom in choosing books, journals or magazines, but comics and pictorial magazines were not allowed. For the minority of pupils, regarded as 'reluctant readers', teachers kept small sets of junior novels in the classroom.

Another 40 percent of the RW students' special time was spent in reading class sets. In the first year, these included junior novels which formed the literature section of the 'traditional' (LLE) course. This section of the course was designed for intensive rather than extensive reading. In discussing the books, terms and concepts developed in the

Oregon Curriculum were used. A little written work was set, but classes did no formal assignments in the first two years. In the third year, however, less emphasis was given to the extensive reading section of the course. There was less 'free' silent reading than in the previous years. Some preparation for outside examinations was undertaken, by requiring students to complete formal prose assignments, sometimes based on typical School Certificate questions. Some class time was spent constructing and discussing model answers, but much of this work was assigned to be done at home.

(b) *Writing*

Approximately 20 percent of the time devoted to special reading and writing was spent in written work. Using Brian Powell's *English Through Poetry Writing*, some time was spent in the first two years on 'creative' writing. This section was taught largely in block form. Early work included exercises on word choice and imagery. This was generally a stimulus for later work on different forms, for example, Ezra Pound Couplets, Haiku, and Dylan Thomas Portraits. Less writing of this sort was done in the second year, and little in the third year of the project, as more time was devoted to structured writing based on intensive reading.

The LLE Course

(a) *Textbooks*

Most of the pupils' study in the LLE course was derived from one of three books by P. R. Smart, *Let's Learn English 3 in the 70s* in Form 3, *Let's Learn English 4* in Form 4, and *Let's Learn English 5* in Form 5.

The third form text is divided into five sections or courses—Language Studies, Reading, Writing, Speaking and Listening, and the Library. The Language Studies course treats language as a communication system and teaches such concepts as registers, signals, context, morphemes, roots, prefixes, and so on. The grammar taught is largely functional and includes the traditional parts of speech (nouns, verbs, adjectives, prepositions, and so on) and the different varieties of phrases and clauses. In this respect it differs markedly from the Transformational Grammar taught in the Oregon Curriculum.

The Reading section includes numerous comprehension exercises, with a wide range of selections culled from newspapers, poetry, myths, narrative, history, novel, exposition—all set within a framework of reading at different speeds for different purposes.

The Writing section presents a variety of exercises designed to appeal to students. Narrative writing receives the main emphasis in Form 3, but reporting, description, dialogue and short story writing are included, along with advice and exercises on paragraphing, diction, sequence, relevance, sentence structure and sentence building.

The Speaking and Listening section deals with group discussion, mime, use of telephone, conversation, formal talks, class meetings, and so on, with relevant practical advice and exercises, while the Library section includes useful information and questions on library catalogues, parts of a book, use of reference books, proper care of books and allied topics.

The unrevised fourth form book in the LLE series, the only edition available at the time, includes major topics similar to those of the third form book, but has additional categories on mass media, vocabulary study, spelling, punctuation and literature. Again a large range of practical exercises is provided, organized in this case, into separate assignments which include specific units from each of the major sections of study—reading, writing, and language.

The fifth form text is more similar to that of the third form in its organization into four main courses, in oral work, reading, writing and language studies. The latter course includes extensive exercises on traditional grammar, including parts of speech, subject and predicate, clause analysis, sentence analysis, and many allied questions designed to prepare students for the School Certificate Examination.

(b) *Teaching Timetable*

In the third form year, students in this course spent approximately three periods of every week on work from the textbook. The teachers adopted a variety of procedures in their approach to each main section of the text, but with regular consultation, it was possible to gain similar emphasis in each class for all of the main skill areas—reading, writing, speaking and listening, and language studies.

Because the fourth form book was arranged as a course textbook more than as a source-book, with each assignment including work on all sections, the students worked through their book more systematically in their fourth form year. Once again, however, modifications and omissions were made by the teachers in consultation. For instance, the work on language studies was left out and the speaking and listening sections were supplemented extensively because more topical material was available.

Timetabling difficulties made it impossible for the two classes in the LLE group to continue to be taught in Form 5 by teachers who had been with them in Forms 3 and 4; instead two experienced and willing members of the staff were assigned to them. Because these teachers did not have an allowance of free time within the provisions of the research project, it was more difficult to keep the two classes exactly parallel. Both classes, however, did spend similar amounts of time on each section of the work so that their pupils can justifiably be combined for the purposes of this investigation. Extracts from *Useful Literacy, Express Yourself, Comprehension, Interpretation and Criticism*, and *School Certificate Revision in English* supplemented the exercises on skills undertaken in *Let's Learn English 5*.

At every level, English was related as often as possible to the experience of the students with discussions, debates and interviews arising out of items of topical interest on television, at school or in the local area.

Regular weekly or fortnightly periods were spent in reading throughout the three years of the course, and students were encouraged to keep a record of their reading.

(c) *Literature in the LLE Course*

Work in Literature occupied about two periods a week in the LLE course. Six to eight class sets already found successful by the teachers were read and discussed each year. Such study centred around the concepts tradition-ally taught in literature, such as *character*, *plot* and *theme*. Teachers of this group were careful not to transfer terms and concepts from the Oregon Curriculum into LLE classes. Poetry from the appropriate volume of *Verse For You* was supplemented by cyclostyled material of the teachers' own choice. In Forms 3 and 4, collaboration between teachers ensured that this additional material was similar in nature and presentation, but the same degree of collaboration did not take place in Form 5. The proportion of time spent on poetry, however, was the same throughout the LLE group in this year.

The treatment of literature in each year varied slightly. In Form 3, for example, six junior novels were studied. These included such books as *The Red Pony*, *Old Mali and the Boy*, *The Silver Sword*, and *The Boy who was Afraid*. They were read mainly for enjoyment, but the teacher tried in each case to give students technical insight into at least one aspect of the novel. In *The Silver Sword*, for example, work in the background or setting was done by the use of project work and of maps and photographs taken in Europe during World War II; in *The Boy who was Afraid*, character development was emphasized. At other times social studies booklets, records, or relevant television programmes were called on to illustrate aspects of the book studied. In the fifth form year more emphasis was placed on the study of the whole work, as well as discussion of the main features of each genre.

Little drama was read in Form 3. In Form 4 two plays were read aloud in class, and this number was increased to three in Form 5. Sometimes, scenes from the plays were produced within the classroom. In the fifth form year, when *Julius Caesar* was studied, the recording of the play was used. In the case of those plays which students found rather removed from their experience, such as *The Importance of Being Earnest*, they were asked to draw contrasts between their immediate environment and the setting of the play. Greater understanding of the plays studied was promoted by having students predict events, or suggest improvements, and sometimes by introducing characters in a role playing situation.

The tables set out below indicate the proportion of time spent in each course on work from the resource textbooks and on literature.

D

Table 5.1

Periods Spent in Each Strand in Each Course

(a) TG Course

	OC Lit.	OC Rhet.	OC TG	Total
1970	85	46	83	214
1971	84	57	75	216
1972	48	49	48	145
Total	217	152	206	575

(b) RW Course

	OC Lit.	OC Rhet.	RW	Total
1970	85	46	83	214
1971	84	57	75	216
1972	48	49	47	144
Total	217	152	205	574

(c) LLE Course

	LLE Text	Lit.	Total
1970	123	86	209
1971	124	92	216
1972	74	75	149
Total	321	253	574

Further time was necessarily occupied with the research evaluation programme. This occupied approximately 14 periods each year, although in the first year, time was taken out of other subject periods as well as those devoted to English. In addition, routine testing for the regular 10-weekly assignments took approximately 12 periods in each year. These schedules were identical for all classes.

6

Tests and Assessment Techniques

The main focus of the research study centred on changes in the essay writing skills of the students taking the contrasting English courses. These skills were central in the minds of the researchers, and were prominent amongst the objectives of the courses studied. However, numerous other tests and assessment procedures were used and these are described below. They were selected either for the initial matching groups, or to detect the presence of other intended or unintended outcomes of the teaching courses. For instance, a course may produce desired increases in composition skills, but if it simultaneously provokes a dislike of writing, or results in poorer reading growth, the improvement in writing may well be seen as unimportant in relation to the students' overall language development. Thus, a wide range of tests and attitude scales was prepared and administered to the students of all groups during each of the three years of the experiment, so that a comprehensive evaluation of each course could be undertaken.

Most of the tests were of general language skills, known or hypothesized to be influenced by English teaching. They included tests of writing, reading comprehension, vocabulary, usage, sentence combining, spelling, listening, English literature, study skills, precis writing and attitudes as well as the School Certificate English Examination.[1] All of these measures were assessing qualities which each of the courses was intended to improve. One additional test, designed to assess the extent of mastery of transformational grammar, was administered to the TG group only, and could not therefore be used for comparison between groups (see Appendix 2).

The first four tests listed below were used as pre-tests, primarily for equating purposes; the remainder were designed for evaluation at the end

1. Samples of the various tests used can be obtained on application to the publisher.

of each year of the course. The pre-tests were administered early in 1970, when the students were newcomers to Form 3; the remainder were administered between September and December, at the end of 1970, 1971, 1972, or 1973.

PRE-TESTS USED FOR EQUATING THE THREE GROUPS
(Form 3, February 1970)

(1)   *General Ability Test (GAT)*[2]

This is the short form of a test of general achievement in basic subjects, prepared by G. L. Arvidson in 1958 from his original three-test battery. It consists of 33 items and has been widely used in New Zealand for classification or guidance purposes at entry to high school. The items test vocabulary, arithmetic, grammar, reading comprehension, spelling, reasoning and general knowledge. Statistical analyses of both long and short forms of the test have shown reliability coefficients over 0.9, and validity coefficients over 0.8, when correlated with third-form examination results,[3] and over 0.7 with School Certificate totals three years later.[4]

(2)   *Progressive Achievement Tests (PAT), Reading Vocabulary, Form C, Part 7*[5]

This is a 65-item test of word knowledge prepared and standardized by the New Zealand Council for Educational Research (NZCER) in 1969. The words are tested in the context of short sentences and in multiple-choice format. The reported reliability coefficients for the Form 3 test are 0.94 (split-half) and 0.91 (equivalent forms) and correlations with comprehension and verbal intelligence tests range from 0.65 to 0.86.

(3)   *Progressive Achievement Tests (PAT), Reading Comprehension, Form C, Part 7*[5]

This test belongs to the same series as the PAT Vocabulary test, and was prepared and standardized by NZCER at the same time. It contains 47 multiple-choice items based on 7 paragraphs of 200-300 words each, covering a wide range of expository and narrative topics. The reliability coefficients of the Part 7 forms range from 0.90 to 0.84 and the median validity coefficient of 13 reported studies is 0.75.

---

2. G. L. Arvidson, *op. cit.*

3. See R. D. McGarvey, 'A Test Battery for Third Form New Entrants', Dip Ed thesis, University of Auckland, 1962.

4. See M. D. Jones, 'Follow-Up Study of A Test Battery for Third Form New Entrants', Dip Ed thesis, University of Auckland, 1967.

5. See W. B. Elley and N. A. Reid, *Progressive Achievement Tests of Reading*, Teachers' Manual (Wellington: NZCER, 1969).

ITEM CHARGED

Patron: Donna Hornik

Patron Barco

2 1 2 2 4 0 5 4 2 5 0 3 0 6

Patron Grou UBReg

Due Date: 8/3/2012 04:30 PM

Title: Role of grammar in a
secondary school
curriculum / W.B. Elley ...
[et al.].

Author:

Call Number: 375.42 E45

Enumeration

Chronology:

Copy: 1

Item Barcode

3 0 3 0 1 0 0 0 7 2 9 3 8 0

(4) *Written Language Test*

This test was prepared at NZCER for the purposes of the experiment. It consists of two parts, named English Usage and Sentence Structure respectively. (1) The English Usage section contains 25 items requiring pupils to correct 'errors' and examples of unacceptable usage in standard written prose. More specifically, it tests such items as agreement of subject and verb forms, appropriate pronouns, detection of double negatives, and so on. (2) The Sentence Structure section contains 25 items testing the ability to identify which one of 4 similar sentences is the most 'correct' and effective expression of an idea.

TESTS AND ASSESSMENT TECHNIQUES USED FOR EVALUATION

(1) Form 3 tests, November–December 1970

In the third form testing programme, pupils were required to write four essays, to take seven objective or semi-objective tests of language skills, and to complete a short questionnaire on their attitudes to English and allied activities. All pupils took the tests at the same time in their normal classrooms between mid-November and early December. No more than one test was administered on each day. The school principal introduced the testing programme to the staff, and the cooperation of 15 teachers was obtained for administering the tests. Considerable lengths were taken to ensure uniformity of administration. Pupils were all acquainted with the purpose of the testing. The objective tests were marked by the English teachers involved in the experiment, and checked at NZCER. Essay marking details are outlined below.

The testing timetable for Form 3 is presented in Table 6.1. In retrospect,

Table 6.1

Form 3 Testing Timetable, November–December 1970

Date	Period	Test
November 17	1	Listening Comprehension
,, 18	3	Essay (i)
,, 19	4	English Usage
,, 20	2	Spelling
,, 23	3	Essay (ii)
,, 24	1	Literature (i)
,, 25	5	Reading Comprehension
,, 26	1	Literature (ii) and (iii)
,, 27	2	Attitude to English
,, 30	1	Essay (iii)
December 1	2	Vocabulary
,, 2	5	Sentence Structure
,, 7	3	Essay (iv)

it was concluded that the programme was somewhat too concentrated, that it could more conveniently have been spread over a longer time span, reduced to a smaller number of tests, and the supervision confined to the three English teachers teaching the experimental classes. These conclusions were acted on in subsequent years.

(a) *Form 3 Essays*

All pupils wrote four essays, approximately one week apart. The pre-tested topics were chosen to enable pupils to write on a diversity of topics to produce different types of writing which could be assessed on a variety of criteria. In the interests of standardization, no choice of subject was given, but each was designed to appeal to all or most of the pupils. No assistance was given by way of prior discussion or help during the test. The topics, as listed below, were written on the blackboard, the purpose of the exercise was explained with appropriate motivation, and instructions were given on time limits (40 minutes). Each pupil was given a code number to ensure that the marker did not know the identity of the pupil.

FORM 3 ESSAY TOPICS

(i) Write a story beginning: 'He saw the gap and decided it was now or never . . .'
(ii) Write an entertaining account entitled 'Breakfast at Our Place'.
(iii) Do you think wild animals should be kept in captivity? Write a speech in which you try to persuade your classmates that your opinion is the opinion they should have too.
(iv) Write a true account for your friends of what you did one Sunday recently.

FORM 3 ESSAY MARKING

Sixteen experienced English teachers from secondary schools in the Auckland area volunteered to make qualitative assessments of the 1,000 essays written. The three teachers involved in the experiment briefed and supervised the markers, but took no active part in the marking. A preliminary meeting was held to explain the purposes of the project, to discuss problems of essay assessment, to agree on criteria for marking each of the four essays, and to mark 'guinea-pig' scripts for practice.

After discussion of relevant research and the needs of the project, it was decided that each essay should be assessed independently by four markers, and that each should make his assessments on four criteria, namely, *content, organization, style* and *mechanics* (see Appendix I for further details). Each marker used a 4-point scale (1–4), for each criterion, and marked on a relative rather than an absolute basis, so that each marker's set of essays had similar proportions of high and low marks on each criterion. The markers read each set of essays four times, making independent assessments for each of the four criteria. Scores were recorded on the mark sheet which was then folded over to conceal the marks on that criterion. Thus the assessment made for content would not influence the assessment for organization and so on. No corrections or marks were made on the papers at all.

As each student wrote four essays, there were 16 independent assessments of each student's writing, and, as each essay was judged on 4 criteria, there were 64 separate judgements made for each student. These marks were subsequently pooled to provide a highly reliable assessment of each student's writing skill, and used as a criterion measure for establishing the reliability of totals obtained from fewer essays and/or markers (see Chapter 10).

All totalling and follow-up analyses of syntactic structures were undertaken later at NZCER.

(b)   *PAT Reading Vocabulary, Form B, Part 8*

See descriptive details above, for Form C, Part 7.

(c)   *PAT Reading Comprehension, Form B, Part 8*

See descriptive details above, for Form C, Part 7.

(d)   *Sentence Combining*

This two-part test was prepared by the teachers and NZCER staff especially for the project. It was presumed that a greater grasp of grammar might be reflected in the ability to perform the kinds of manipulations required to join and restructure sentences. In Part I (18 items) pupils were to select which one of four given sentences 'best' combined the content of three or four short sentences. Pupils were asked to choose the answer which preserved the original meaning, and was the most concise and correct. Part II consisted of 12 open-ended questions. Pupils had to join pairs of short related sentences in two different ways, without using 'and'; for example, *Tom Jones is a pop-singer* and *Tom Jones is admired by the girls.* These sentences could be combined as follows:

  (i) Tom Jones is a pop-singer who is admired by the girls.
 (ii) The girls admire Tom Jones, who is a pop-singer.
(iii) Tom Jones, who is a pop-singer, is admired by the girls.

(e)   *English Usage*

This was a two-part test parallel to the written language test used for matching at the beginning of 1970. Part A contains 25 items, requiring students to correct 'errors' in a selection of continuous prose. Part B contains 25 multiple-choice items. Students select from four similar sentences the one which expresses an idea most effectively and without grammatical 'error'.

(f) *Spelling*

This was a specifically prepared test of 50 words ranging in difficulty from easy to hard. They were drawn from a variety of tests and included only commonly used words. Some were known to be of special difficulty, for example, *privilege, accommodation, rhythm.* Each word was pronounced by the teacher in isolation, and in the context of a short sentence. The test was included because it was hypothesized that those who read more widely might have gained more in spelling skills due to a greater exposure to words.

(g) *PAT Listening Comprehension, Form A, Part 8*[6]

This is a 45-item test of listening skills, prepared and standardized by NZCER in 1971. Eight short passages on various topics, are read to the pupils by their teacher. After each passage, pupils answer multiple-choice questions for which the possible answer options are displayed in their books. Reported reliability coefficients for the test range from 0.78 to 0.96, and validity coefficients for the series show figures ranging from 0.68 to 0.82 when the tests are correlated with other tests of listening comprehension.

(h) *Literature*

This three-part test was designed to assess literary understanding and appreciation. The selections used were new to the pupils.

   (i) Fiction: Pupils were asked to read a selection of 1,800 words by Edgar Allen Poe, 'The Tell-Tale Heart', and to answer 19 multiple-choice questions on literary appreciation.

   (ii) Poetry: Pupils were required to read 'The Line-Gang' by Robert Frost, and to answer 12 multiple-choice questions testing imagery, understanding, use of language, purpose, and so on.

   (iii) Fiction: This part was adapted from a Literature Test used in the IEA survey.[7] Pupils were asked to read a story of 1,400 words by Ray Bradbury, 'I See You Never', and to answer 18 multiple-choice questions thereon.

(i) *Attitudes to English*

This three-part questionnaire was prepared at NZCER, with the help of the participating teachers. It was designed to assess the pupils' attitudes to reading, to various parts of English as a school subject, and to ascertain the children's general reading preferences. The questionnaire was given anonymously to ensure a greater degree of frankness and sincerity. The three parts were as follows:

   (i) Pupils were asked to rank 'Reading' as one of eight popular leisure-time activities, including TV viewing, films, sports, and riding a bicycle.

6. See W. B. Elley and N. A. Reid, *Progressive Achievement Tests, Listening Comprehension,* Teacher's Manual (Wellington: NZCER, 1971).

7. A. C. Purves, *Literature Education in Ten Countries* (London: Wiley, International Association for the Evaluation of Educational Achievement (IEA), 1973).

(ii) All compulsory school subjects were listed, and pupils were asked to rank them in relation to reading, writing and grammar.

(iii) Pupils were asked to indicate their reading preferences, by ranking in order six general categories of reading materials—annuals, comics, fiction, non-fiction, magazines and poetry.

(2)   Form 4 Tests, September–November 1971

In the fourth form testing programme, pupils were required to write three essays, to take five objective or semi-objective tests of language skills, and to complete a questionnaire designed to reveal attitudes to various facets of their English programme, and of school in general. This programme was less arduous than that of the third-form year. Test administration was readily standardized for all classes, as it was confined to the three participating teachers. Procedures for setting, collecting and marking the tests were generally the same as in the previous year. No formal listening tests were given in the fourth form, as the third form testing programme had shown that they were unlikely to produce significant differences. The spelling test was also omitted, as it was felt that a sufficiently sensitive measure of this skill could be obtained from the students' essay writing. The attitude scale was changed and extended to provide a more comprehensive picture of specific aspects of the English courses, and other tests were modified according to the experience gained in the previous year's programme.

The testing programme for Form 4 is outlined in Table 6.2.

Table 6.2
Form 4 Testing Timetable, September–November 1971

Date	Period	Test
September 16	3–4	Reading Comprehension
,, 22	3–4	Essay (i)
,, 28	4–5	English Usage
,, 30	3–4	Vocabulary
October 5	4–5	Essay (ii)
,, 7	3–4	Attitudes
,, 13	3–4	Literature (i)
,, 19	4–5	Essay (iii)
,, 26	4–5	Sentence Combining
November 2	3–4	Literature (ii)

(a)   *Form 4 Essays*

One outcome of the analysis of third form results was the discovery that the use of four essays and four markers for each pupil produced total results which were no more reliable than would have been obtained from three essays and two markers (see Chapter 10). Therefore in their fourth form year, the students were asked to write only three essays and these were read by only two different markers. The topics for the 1971 series are listed below.

FORM 4 ESSAY TOPICS

(i) Write an account, for a cousin in Australia, describing the suburb or community you live in. You could include such things as the sorts of people who live in the community, the buildings, the recreational facilities, and so on. You may, if you like, concentrate on only one or two features that you consider will be of most interest.

(ii) Do you think that household pets should be banned in towns and cities? Persuade your classmates that your opinion is the right one.

(iii) Write an interesting account for the other members of your class on: What I (or my family) did at Labour weekend. You could write about one incident, one day, or the whole weekend.

FORM 4 ESSAY MARKING

After thorough briefing and extensive 'guinea-pig' marking, six experienced English teachers, all of whom had assisted in 1970, undertook the marking of the essays. The briefing notes for markers contained useful advice on factors shown to influence markers' subjective opinions and the briefing sessions occupied over an hour on each of the three days of marking. Each essay was marked independently by two different markers, and the essays were so arranged that one sample of each pupil's writing was marked by each of the six markers. Precautions were also taken to ensure that no pupil had his essays marked consistently at the beginning or end of the marking sessions. The criteria used in assessing the essays are detailed in Appendix 1.

(b) *PAT Reading Comprehension, Form A, Part 8*

See descriptive details above, for Form C, Part 7.

(c) *PAT Reading Vocabulary, Form A, Part 8*

See descriptive details above for Form C, Part 7.

(d) *Sentence Combining*

This test consisted of 30 sets of 3 or 4 short sentences each of which is to be combined by the students into one well-constructed sentence, without the use of 'and'.

For example:

Bernard has an elaborate chemistry set.

His interest in science is well-known.

The chemistry set must not be interfered with.

In each set, the students were given guidance on how to begin the new sentence so that they would be required to use a variety of transformations.

(e) *Usage*

This was a 29-item test based on a passage of continuous prose and was similar in content to the corresponding test used in Form 3. Certain lines contained 'errors' in verb tense, number, word choice, word order and other common faults. The students' task was to identify and correct these errors.

(f) *English Literature*

This was a two-part test designed to measure literary understanding and appreciation.

    (i) Fiction: Pupils read a short story, 'The Use of Force', by William Carlos Williams, and answered 22 questions on literary appreciation.[8]

    (ii) Poetry: Two short poems were selected for reading, 'View of a Pig' by Ted Hughes and 'Death of a Whale' by John Blight, and, after trial testing with open-ended questions, a set of 15 objective questions was prepared on such aspects of literature as the poets' word choice, their attitudes to their subject and the contrast between the poems.

(g) *Attitudes to English*

The pupils' attitudes were assessed by means of a 5 part questionnaire, filled in anonymously, in the interests of greater honesty on the part of the pupils.

In Part One the pupils were asked to indicate the extent of their agreement with statements about how well they had progressed in 12 aspects of English, since coming to their school. Example statements referred to amount of reading, improvement in essays, interest in words, ability to organize their ideas, and so on. The students' agreement with these statements was indicated by recording a tick on a 5 point scale, ranging from 'Strongly Agree' to 'Strongly Disagree'.

Part Two assessed the students' attitudes to 20 specific English activities, using a 5 point scale ranging from 'Like Very Much' to 'Dislike Very Much'. The activities rated included reading of different kinds of materials, writing for various purposes, sentence study, discussion, textbooks, and so on.

Part Three required the pupils to rank English, in relation to other subjects of their curriculum in Form 4, whereas Parts Four and Five sought the pupils' general attitude to English and to school respectively, by asking them to tick, in each case, one of five statements expressing degree of like or dislike.

---

8. Adapted from the IEA test in *Literature and Education in Ten Countries, op. cit.*

(3) **Form 5 Tests, August–November 1972**

In the fifth form testing programme, pupils were required to write four essays, to take six objective or semi-objective tests of various language skills, and to complete a lengthy questionnaire designed to assess their attitudes to different aspects of their English study.

The general organization and administration of the testing was similar to that conducted in Form 4. An additional test was introduced to assess certain study skills which might have been affected by the differential experience of the groups in reading and library work, and further indices of ability in English were obtained from the School Certificate Examination in English, which all the pupils took in November 1972. New approaches were introduced in the assessment of attitudes, and the essay writing was extended to allow all pupils to write again on one of the topics they had chosen in their Form 3 essay testing.

The testing programme for Form 5 is outlined in Table 6.3.

Table 6.3

Form 5 Testing Timetable, August–November 1972

Date	Period	Test
August 15	4–5	Study Skills
September 12	4–5	Vocabulary
„ 14	3–4	Essay (i)
„ 20	3–4	Attitudes
„ 26	4–5	Essay (ii)
„ 28	3–4	Reading Comprehension
October 3	4–5	English Usage
„ 5	3–4	Literature (i)
„ 24	4–5	Literature (ii)
„ 25	3–4	Essay (iii)
„ 31	4–5	Literature (iii)
November 2	3–4	Sentence Structure
„ 8	3–4	Essay (iv)

(a) *Form 5 Essays*

Four essays were written by the pupils in the third term of 1972, for the purposes of the research study. The first three were written by all pupils, and are listed below. The fourth offered pupils a choice of one of the four topics on which they had written in the third form year. Thus it was possible to measure the extent of growth on several writing criteria over a period of two years. The conditions under which the pupils wrote their essays were similar to those of Forms 3 and 4.

FORM 5 ESSAY TOPICS

    (i) 'My Candidate for the School Council'. Describe your choice and try to persuade others to vote for your candidate.

    (ii) Read the following extract from the *New Zealand Herald*, 8 September 1972.

Death Every 45 Minutes

A fiercely argued debate here on the psychological impact on viewers of television violence has confronted the public with this information:

That the average New Zealander between his second and sixty-fifth year spends 3,000 entire days (nearly nine years of his life) simply sitting watching TV;

That by the time a five-year-old child in New Zealand enters school, he has already spent more time learning about the world from the family TV set than is spent by a BA student in a classroom throughout his university years;

That what both the adult and the child are watching all this time are programmes containing (according to a recent average week) an incident of violence every 14 minutes and a killing every three-quarters of an hour.

These staggering facts have emerged from evidence presented to the Royal Commission on the Causes and Prevention of Violence.

Express your reaction to and opinions on the issues presented in this newspaper report in detail. Be as clear and logical as you can.

    (iii) 'An Unpleasant Experience'

    (iv) In the fourth essay pupils chose one of the four topics on which they had written in their third form year (see p 42).

FORM 5 ESSAY MARKING

Marking was undertaken in the same manner as in the previous year, with the aid of six experienced English teachers. In order to assess the amount of pupil progress in writing since the third form year, the essays for both third and fifth form, written by the same pupils on the same topic, were mixed together, after coding, and the markers asked to assess them in the usual way. All the essays were written in ink on the same paper, purchased in bulk in 1970, so that it would not be easy for the markers to determine which were third and which fifth form essays. Precautions were taken to ensure that both essays by each pupil were marked by the same markers, although never in the same batch of essays. Afterwards the essays were re-sorted into third and fifth form sets for separate analysis and comparison.

(b)   *Reading Comprehension*

As the PAT series was not designed for fifth form classes, it was decided to use the more difficult passages from a fourth form Test (Part 8, Form C) and to add another passage with seven questions, adapted from an

English test prepared at NZCER for the sixth form level. The final test contained 38 items, and the results obtained showed that it is comparable to the other PAT Comprehension Tests in reliability and validity.

(c) *PAT Reading Vocabulary, Form C, Part 8*

See descriptive details above, for Form C, Part 7. The fourth form test was used in this case because it was found to have enough 'ceiling' to spread out even the best pupils in the experiment.

(d) *Sentence Combining*

This test of 26 items was parallel to, but slightly more difficult than, the corresponding test for Form 4. Some of the sets of sentences to be combined contained as many as six kernel sentences. Again, the students were given the starting word or phrase.

(e) *English Usage*

This test consisted of 38 items based on separate sentences requiring correction of 'errors' in formal written language. The sentences were culled directly, or adapted, from the students' essays, after a searching analysis. The exercises therefore exemplify the kinds of problems which are common at this level; for example, run-on sentences, use of capitals, apostrophes, commas, contractions, and so on.

(f) *Study Skills*

This was an objective test, of 52 items, prepared at NZCER, largely by adapting items from overseas tests and pretesting on children at neighbouring schools. There were items on terms in common use in the library, the use of an index, an encyclopedia, a dictionary, arranging items in alphabetical order, and allied topics.

(g) *English Literature*

This was a three-part test designed to measure literary understanding and appreciation.

   (i) Fiction: Pupils read a short story, 'After You, My Dear Alphonse', by Shirley Jackson, and answered 15 questions, 7 of which were multiple-choice, and 8 open-ended. The questions asked about the attitudes, motives, beliefs, relationships, and tones of voice of the characters, what message the story contained, and similar topics.

   (ii) Poetry: Pupils read a short poem, 'The Cosmetic Counter', by Peter Bland, and answered 15 questions, mostly multiple-choice, on its meaning, symbolism and imagery, and the poet's purpose and attitude.

   (iii) Poetry: Pupils read another short poem, 'The Cow', by John Ciardi, and answered 10 open-ended questions thereon. The emphasis of the questions was on the literal and underlying meaning of the poem.

(h)   *Attitudes to English*

The pupils' attitudes were assessed in a four-part questionnaire admini-stered to all groups.

In the first part, students listed the subjects they took in the fifth form, wrote a sentence or two about their attitude towards each, and ranked the subjects in order of preference.

Part two used the 'semantic differential' method to determine the students' attitudes towards five aspects of English—writing essays, literature, reading, language textbook and sentence study. In this method the students were asked to rate each concept on 14 different dimensions, described by pairs of bi-polar adjectives. Example dimensions were Pleasant-Unpleasant, Difficult-Easy, Useless-Useful, Imaginative-Unimaginative, and so on. The rating was done by circling a number on a seven-point scale, in accordance with the students' feelings.

The questions were set out as in the example below:

	Writing Essays							
Pleasant	1	2	3	4	5	6	7	*Unpleasant*
Difficult	1	1	3	4	5	6	7	*Easy*

This approach to assessing attitudes has been widely used overseas, and has proved a sensitive index for 'mapping' the connotative meanings which respondents attach to the concepts rated.[9]

Part three of the questionnaire required the students to rate on a five-point scale, their attitudes towards their own progress in the fifth form on a variety of activities in English, and part four assessed the students' liking or dislike of different aspects of English. These two parts were very similar to the corresponding sections of the fourth form questionnaire.

(i)   TRANSFORMATIONAL GRAMMAR

In order to assess the mastery of TG grammar, the TG group was given a set of sentences to analyse according to the principles they had learned. This test and its results are described in greater detail in Appendix 2.

(4)   Sixth Form Follow-up Test

The project was officially terminated at the end of the fifth form year in December 1972. At that point, many of the participating pupils left school, some were required to repeat their fifth form courses, while those who proceeded to the sixth form took a variety of courses. It was therefore impossible to control the contents of their English classes in the manner of their first three years. Nevertheless, it was felt that a follow-up test, designed to assess the students' writing skills, may well throw further light on the long-term effects of the different English courses.

9. See C. E. Osgood, G. J. Suci and P. H. Tannenbaum, *The Measurement of Meaning* (Urbana: University of Illinois Press, 1957).

The results of earlier years had suggested that those pupils studying grammar might be demonstrating a marginal superiority in their control over sentence structure in the sentence combining and usage tests, although this superiority was definitely not reflected in their written essays. To explore this matter further, it was decided to give students a précis exercise. This kind of writing offers more constraints than a typical essay, but enough freedom to enable the students to demonstrate their writing style. Thus, the pupils were required to rewrite a 300 word extract on oil exploration in Alaska in a short statement of 100–120 words. These were marked by English teachers from other schools in the same manner as the essays of previous years, except that the 'content' criterion was omitted. Subsequently the précis exercises were analysed at NZCER on more objective criteria.

7

Analysis of Results

To compare the effects of the three English programmes, test results and attitude scores were obtained at the end of the pupils' third form, fourth form and fifth form years, with some follow-up data at the end of the sixth form. The results of the main comparisons are presented below, separately for each class level. Each variable was checked for abnormal distribution before analyses were undertaken. For the most part, the comparisons of means were made by t tests or analyses of variance, except where the data required non-parametric statistics.

THIRD FORM RESULTS

(1) Test Scores

Table 7.1 presents the means and standard deviations on all tests and essays for the pupils in all three English programmes at the end of Form 3, when the experiment had been proceeding for almost a year. The four essay scores were combined to produce one total, but the sub-totals are also shown for the four marking criteria used by the sixteen markers. As described previously, all essays were assessed by four different markers, each applying the four criteria of mechanics, style, structure and content. Since each assessment was made on a four-point scale, the possible score for the Essay Total was 4 x 4 x 4 x 4, or 256.

Inspection of the table indicates that on none of the 12 variables did any English programme show a significant superiority. Only two mean differences were greater than two points, in Essay Total and Sentence Combining, but neither approached a statistically significant level. At the end of one year then, the three programmes produced no observable

E

The Role of Grammar

differences in any of the language skills of reading, writing or listening, nor in English literature.

Similar analyses were undertaken to determine whether any of the three teachers produced higher mean scores than the others on any of the twelve variables. Once again no significant differences were obtained on any test.

Table 7.1

Means and Standard Deviations on 12 Variables for Pupils in 3 English Programmes—End of Form 3

Programme N		TG 91	RW 88	LLE 61
Essay Total	M	160.37	161.08	157.57
	SD	31.43	26.18	31.84
Reading Vocabulary	M	46.62	47.19	47.12
	SD	10.08	9.05	8.76
Reading Comprehension	M	26.52	27.59	27.65
	SD	6.08	6.06	6.77
Sentence Combining	M	31.16	29.08	30.50
	SD	5.67	6.57	6.22
English Usage	M	25.16	24.52	24.26
	SD	5.50	5.82	5.57
Spelling	M	20.47	19.80	20.83
	SD	10.20	10.35	9.64
Listening Comprehension	M	27.60	28.25	27.87
	SD	6.01	5.39	5.10
English Literature	M	26.52	27.74	26.56
	SD	6.08	5.08	5.70
Essay Mechanics	M	42.40	41.44	41.54
	SD	9.87	8.93	9.90
Essay Style	M	39.20	39.44	37.72
	SD	8.86	7.14	8.94
Essay Structure	M	40.29	41.43	40.00
	SD	7.72	6.47	7.69
Essay Content	M	38.25	38.74	38.44
	SD	7.63	6.78	8.19

(2) Attitudes

Three questions were asked in the attitude scale given at the end of the third form year.

(a) *Ranking of Reading as a Leisure Time Interest*

In this question pupils were asked to rank nine leisure-time interests, amongst which reading was included. The median rankings for the TG, RW, and LLE groups respectively, were 4.82, 5.08 and 5.36, and the differences between them were not significant. Reading was consistently less popular than outdoor sports, TV and listening to records, across all groups. A check was also made for differences between the classes taught by the three teachers, regardless of their course. Again, no significant differences were found.

(b)   *Ranking of School Subjects*

In this section of the questionnaire, pupils ranked six school subjects according to how well they liked them. The overall results as presented in Table 7.2 showed social studies to be the most popular, followed by reading, science, mathematics, writing and grammar, in that order. The RW group showed a marginally greater liking for reading than the TG group ($\chi^2=13.20$, $p< 0.05$) and both RW and LLE groups liked writing more than the TG group ($\chi^2=25.68$ $p<0.01$), but no other differences appeared either in the between-course comparisons in English, or in the between-teacher comparisons. Overall, the differences between courses in this section appear to have been more marked than those between teachers.

Table 7.2
Median Ranking of School Subjects—End of Form 3

Subject	TG	RW	LLE
Social Studies	2.78	2.24	2.42
Reading	3.30	2.79	3.10
Mathematics	3.01	3.21	4.69
Science	3.28	4.17	2.61
Writing	4.38	3.79	3.77
Grammar	4.22	4.68	4.29

(c)   *Ranking of Preferred Reading Materials*

For this question pupils ranked the main categories of reading materials according to preference. The pattern for the total group showed that the most popular materials were fiction, followed by magazines, comics, non-fiction, annuals and poetry, in that order. No significant differences appeared between English programmes or teachers in these patterns.

FOURTH FORM RESULTS

(1)   **Test Scores**

It will be recalled that the fourth form test programme was reduced to five language tests, three essays and one attitude scale. Each of the essays was marked by two independent markers on the same four criteria as were used in the third form testing programme. The fourth form test

The Role of Grammar

results for all three English courses are set out in Table 7.3. Of the 30 possible comparisons which could be drawn on these criteria, only one proved statistically significant, that between the RW and LLE group on the Essay-Content criterion ($F=4.74$, $p<0.01$). As one would expect an occasional difference of this magnitude to arise by chance in such a large number of tests, and as a corresponding pattern was not found in the third or fifth form results on the Essay Content criterion, it could safely be concluded that this is a chance difference. Certainly it was not a hypothesized difference. In other words, the fourth form results confirm those found at the end of the third form. There were no apparent differences between the three groups in any language abilities after the different programmes had been in operation for a period of two years.

In order to explore the data further, a series of two-way analyses of variance was undertaken, in which the differences in scores attributable to the three teachers were compared with those due to the English programmes. On two essay criteria (mechanics and content) and on the sentence-combining test, one teacher produced significantly better results than the other two at the 0.05 level. A study of the scores on the matching variables of those pupils remaining at the end of Form 4, however, showed that the

Table 7.3

*Means and Standard Deviations for 3 English Programmes
on 10 Tests—End of Form 4*

Programme N		TG 71	RW 75	LLE 49
Essay Total	M	61.21	59.79	63.69
	SD	13.05	11.96	14.66
Reading Vocabulary	M	42.92	44.35	43.94
	SD	9.65	8.53	8.58
Reading Comprehension	M	30.15	31.32	30.82
	SD	7.88	6.20	6.41
Sentence Combining	M	16.04	14.48	14.52
	SD	7.32	6.20	6.74
English Usage	M	10.59	10.88	11.20
	SD	3.44	3.17	2.78
English Literature	M	21.55	21.25	21.80
	SD	4.59	4.17	3.85
Essay Mechanics	M	16.40	16.27	16.51
	SD	3.03	3.06	4.71
Essay Style	M	15.86	14.53	15.43
	SD	3.71	3.49	4.20
Essay Structure	M	15.52	15.47	15.61
	SD	3.86	3.58	3.83
Essay Content	M	14.90	14.38*	16.06*
	SD	4.00	3.09	3.35

* Denotes significant difference (see text).

same teacher had a slightly brighter group of pupils at that stage in the experiment. As the differences between these effects due to teachers were very small, and as no interactions were found to be significant, they were not felt to be important. They could not have produced any distorting effects in the comparisons between programmes.

(2) Attitudes

The attitude questionnaire administered at the end of the fourth form contained five parts. The results are presented separately below.

(a) *Part 1: Progress in English*

This section contained 12 questions in which pupils rated, on a 5-point scale, the extent to which they agreed with statements about their progress in various aspects of their English programme. Figure 7.1 shows that for 6 of the 36 possible t tests, the differences between programmes were significant at the 0.05 level. Briefly, the pattern which emerges from these figures is that the TG pupils believed that they read less than they used to, and that English was harder for them, a reflection, perhaps, on their time spent on transformational grammar. They also believed that they found it easier than the RW group to arrange their ideas in their writing. There is, unfortunately, no evidence in the essay results to support this latter opinion. On the criteria of structure and mechanics, RW pupils were writing just as well as the other groups.

The results also showed that, by contrast with the RW group, LLE pupils believed their essays to have improved in several respects. Again there was no objective evidence in the essay scores to support their conclusion.

An analysis of differences between teacher effects produced 8 (out of a possible 36) significant differences. These differences were confined to 4 questions—enjoyment of essays, improvement in essays, writing in longer sentences, and finding English easier—and 7 of the 8 favoured one teacher. Interestingly enough, this was not the same teacher who produced the significantly better results in essay writing as assessed by the teachers.

There is a strong suggestion in these data that attitudes towards, and beliefs about progress in English, may be influenced more by certain qualities of the teacher than by the English programmes, but that these attitudes are not reflected in the pupils' actual performance. Discrepancies of this kind between self-ratings and those made by others, on more objective criteria, seem to require further study.

Other noticeable trends from the results in Part I were the relative unpopularity of poetry and essay writing. Few pupils saw improvement in their feelings here. Most of the pupils believed that they read more at high school, and understood more of what they read, and most felt that their essays had improved a little.

58   *The Role of Grammar*

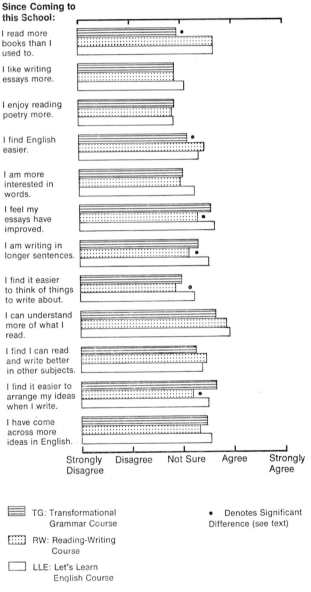

Since Coming to this School:

Strongly Disagree — Disagree — Not Sure — Agree — Strongly Agree

TG: Transformational Grammar Course
RW: Reading-Writing Course
LLE: Let's Learn English Course

• Denotes Significant Difference (see text)

Figure 7.1 *Progress in English—Form 4*

(b) *Part 2*: *Liking for English*

This section contained 19 questions in which pupils rated, on a 5-point scale, the extent to which they liked or disliked various activities in their English programmes. The overall pattern revealed in Figure 7.2 shows a general liking for oral discussion, reading and imaginative writing, and a corresponding dislike for poetry, in any shape or form, and for sentence study. The Oregon Curriculum groups showed obvious liking for their literature textbook, but the language and rhetoric sections did not generate enthusiasm in any group.

Of the 57 possible differences between programmes in this section of the questionnaire, only 8 were statistically significant, and most of these barely reached significance at the 0.05 level. The Oregon groups showed a greater liking for explanatory and persuasive writing than the LLE pupils, a finding which was interpreted by the teachers in terms of the very effective treatment of these kinds of writing in the Oregon rhetoric strand. The only large difference appearing in this section of the questionnaire occurred in the strong positive attitude of the TG group towards the Oregon Literature textbook. This finding may reflect the strong contrast the TG pupils felt between their literature and grammar texts, a contrast which was not applicable in the case of the other two groups. The remaining differences were small and not easy to interpret, and were probably chance fluctuations.

The comparisons between teachers in this section produced 17 significant differences, out of a possible 57, but none of them was dramatic. One teacher produced a more positive attitude towards writing in five comparisons, one engendered a liking for poetry, and a corresponding dislike for letter writing, and the third teacher produced favourable attitudes to letter writing, but more unfavourable attitudes towards other kinds of writing and to the textbooks. These results reflect no doubt the various enthusiasms and strengths of the three teachers. Such factors are unlikely to have affected comparisons between programmes, however, as the teachers had a similar amount of time with each class.

(c) *Part 3*: *Ranking of English in Relation to Other Subjects*

In this section, the pupils were asked to rank the school subjects according to their preference for each. The four subjects taken by all pupils were English, mathematics, science and social studies. Overall, English was ranked just below the middle point on the scale, and the differences between the programmes were negligible, the median ranks being 2.45, 2.38 and 2.34 for the TG, RW and LLE groups respectively. A between-teacher comparison showed that one teacher produced significantly more favourable attitudes to English than the other two ($\chi^2=9.15$, $p<0.05$, and $\chi^2=20.63$, $p<0.01$) and thus corroborated the results obtained in Part I of this questionnaire.

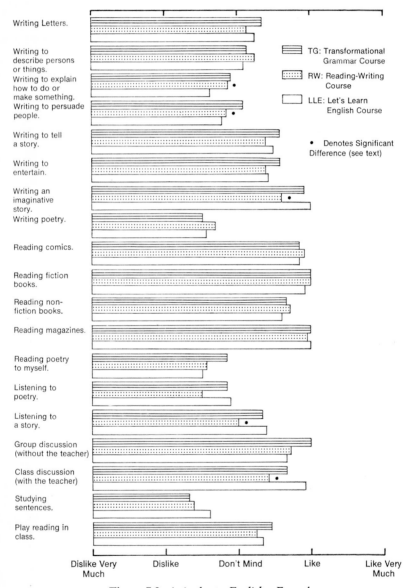

Figure 7.2 *Attitudes to English—Form 4*

(d)   *Part 4*: *Feelings about English*

Pupils evaluated their overall attitude towards English by checking one of five statements which most nearly represented their feelings. A chi square test showed no difference between programmes, but one teacher produced significantly more positive attitudes ($\chi^2 = 15.64$, $p < 0.01$) than one other, again confirming the results of other sections of the questionnaire about this teacher.

(e)   *Part 5*: *Attitude towards School*

Pupils assessed their general attitude towards school by checking one of five statements that most nearly represented their opinion. All groups revealed an attitude slightly lower than the mid-point on the scale, and none of the differences between programmes or teachers proved significant.

FIFTH FORM RESULTS

(1)   Test Scores

Table 7.4 sets out the means and standard deviations on all tests for the 164 pupils who remained in the investigation at the end of the fifth form. Once again the four essays were combined into one total score, and broken down also according to the four marking criteria. As most of the pupils took the School Certificate English examination their results are also included.

Of the 12 variables listed in Table 7.4, only 2 showed significant F ratios in the Analysis of Variance, the Sentence Combining Test ($F = 3.23$, $p < 0.05$) and the English Usage Test ($F = 3.99$, $p < 0.02$). In order to clarify these differences, follow-up Newman-Keulls tests were undertaken. These showed that both the TG and the RW groups scored significantly better than the LLE group in Sentence Combining exercises, the former at the 0.01 level, the latter at the 0.05 level. On the English Usage Test, the TG and LLE groups both produced means significantly higher at the 0.05 level than the RW group. In no other cases, not even the 3-hour School Certificate Examination, did any group show any advantage over the others.

As the two differences that were found were marginal, a closer analysis was made of these results in order to pinpoint their exact nature. Two-way analyses of variance were conducted on all variables, contrasting programmes with sex, and then with level of ability. The analyses by sex revealed that girls produced significantly and uniformly superior results on both Sentence Combining and Usage tests on all three programmes. There were no significant interactions, however ($p = 0.80$ and 0.33). The groups were then subdivided into two levels according to general ability, as measured by Arvidson's General Ability Test. Once again there were no significant interactions on the two tests in question ($p = 0.17$ and 0.08).

Table 7.4

Means and Standard Deviations for Pupils in 3 English Programmes on 12 Variables—End of Form 5

Programme N		TG 60	RW 62	LLE 42
Essay Total	M	79.69	78.40	78.83
	SD	17.58	15.21	16.35
Reading Vocabulary	M	50.43	50.51	49.89
	SD	7.43	7.50	7.08
Reading Comprehension	M	22.85	23.35	22.94
	SD	5.79	5.32	5.25
Sentence Combining	M	13.42*	12.81*	11.00*
	SD	5.36	4.36	5.42
English Usage	M	20.47*	17.69*	20.24*
	SD	6.32	5.83	6.93
English Literature	M	23.15	22.71	22.40
	SD	4.87	4.50	4.79
Study Skills	M	30.48	28.76	28.14
	SD	6.30	6.17	6.09
S.C. English Examination	M	47.80	47.90	46.80
	SD	14.70	11.10	12.30
Essay Mechanics	M	21.49	20.45	20.93
	SD	6.21	5.48	6.02
Essay Style	M	19.59	19.64	19.45
	SD	5.87	5.21	5.74
Essay Structure	M	19.60	19.45	19.50
	SD	5.03	5.97	6.01
Essay Content	M	19.21	18.90	18.98
	SD	6.14	5.09	5.42

* Denotes significant differences (see text).

The TG high-ability group performed slightly better than the other high-ability groups on the six tests, but in no case were the differences statistically significant. Thus there was no evidence in these data that girls, or brighter pupils, benefit more from a study of grammar than other pupils.

An item analysis was then carried out to determine whether the significant differences found were general, or were specific to one or two kinds of questions, or were related to speed of work. On the Sentence Combining Test, the LLE group had the lowest percentage correct on 25 of the 26 items, and in 15 of these items the margin was at least 10 percent. These items were spread throughout the test. Clearly the difference was in no way specific to one or two items. The two Oregon groups thus showed a slight superiority (9.3 percent and 6.9 percent) over the LLE pupils in the general skills of joining, manipulating and restructuring sentences.

In the English Usage Test the TG pupils performed better than the RW group on 28 of the 38 items and the discrepancy was at least 10 percent on

16 of these. In no case did the RW group exceed the TG pupils by 10 percent. An analysis of the items revealing the largest differences in favour of the TG group showed that they were spread over a variety of minor mechanical problems. Two were concerned with the use of capitals, 3 with commas in parenthetical statements, 2 with commas in lists, 3 with spelling (quiet=quite, of=off, alot), 1 for the use of apostrophe, 1 comma in an appositional statement, and 2 run-on sentences. Yet 7 of the questions had specifically tested run-on sentences, where the TG group might be expected to have performed better. If the transformational grammar had developed any superiority in matters of conventional usage—and it was only a slight advantage of 2.8 points in a 38-item test (7.3 percent)—its superiority was confined to rather trivial mechanical faults, and not to sensitivity to sentence structure.

The LLE mean score was 2.5 points (6.6 percent) higher than the RW mean, and an analysis of the differences in items showed a similar trend to that found in the case of the TG pupils. The LLE group performed better by 12 percent or more on capital letters (2 items), punctuation (4), spelling (1), contraction (1), and run-on sentences (2).

A further check was made of the performance of all three groups on the 7 items testing run-on sentences. On average, the TG and LLE pupils scored higher than the RW group by 11.4 percent and 8.6 percent respectively. In neither case was the figure significantly higher than the percentage over all items (7.3 percent and 6.6 percent). What slight superiority there was in the two grammar groups was dispersed over a wide range of mechanical conventions, and was not clearly associated with sentence structure.

To assess the effects of teachers in the test scores of their pupils, a two-way analysis of variance contrasting teachers and programmes was conducted. Only the TG and RW groups were included in the analysis in order that effects due to all three teachers could be determined.

Of the 12 variables examined, only the English Usage test showed a significant difference between teachers ($F=7.31$, $p<0.001$). However, the differences attributable to the one teacher concerned were found to occur in similar fashion in both classes and the F ratio for interaction between teachers and programmes was only 0.67. In other words the significant difference found between programmes in the previous analysis could not be attributed to differences between teachers.

(2) Attitudes

The fifth form attitude questionnaire consisted of five sections which explored the students' attitudes and opinions about various aspects of their English courses.

(a) *Part 1: General Attitude to School Subjects*

Pupils were asked to list the five subjects they were taking in their School Certificate programme, to write down their likes and dislikes about each subject, and then to rank them in order of preference. Main interest centred on the ranking given to English. The median rankings for the three programmes were 2.65, 2.91 and 2.92 for the TG, RW and LLE groups respectively. As for the previous two years, there were no significant differences between the groups in the overall attitude to English when questioned in this manner. It is worthy of note, in passing, that of the 9 subjects taken by 25 or more pupils, English ranked third, after the 2 practical subjects, Engineering and Technical Drawing. The average rankings for all subjects are listed in Table 7.5.

Table 7.5
Median Rankings of Preferences for Fifth Form Subjects

Subject	TG	RW	LLE	Total	Total N
English	2.65	2.91	2.92	2.82	171
Science	3.46	3.33	3.19	3.33	87
Mathematics	3.91	3.64	3.73	3.75	141
Geography	2.89	3.19	2.73	2.96	136
History	3.13	3.64	3.14	3.27	41
Technical Drawing	2.68	2.29	2.00	2.32	63
Biology	3.67	3.11	4.00	3.54	26
Accounting	4.36	3.53	3.50	3.76	38
Engineering	1.82	2.00	1.75	1.86	29

To investigate these general attitudes further, an analysis was made of the students' open-ended statements about English. As a list of illustrative adjectives and comments had been provided in the questionnaire, it was not surprising that many students chose to use these comments in their general summing-up of their subjects. Favourable and unfavourable comments were tabulated and counted. Where students made both positive and negative comments, they were tabulated separately.

The overall pattern indicated a positive attitude on the whole, as 131 out of 211 statements made (62.1 percent) were classified as favourable. The most popular positive comments used were 'interesting', 'useful' and 'variety'; the most common negative comments were 'boring', 'repetitive' and 'difficult'. In some cases, the comments referred to specific aspects of the course—'too many essays', or 'literature helps understand people', or 'grammar useless'. In many cases, however, the statements were vague, and some could not be regarded as evaluative. This kind of analysis is therefore necessarily subjective, but can supplement the questionnaire results in a revealing way.

Some differences between groups were apparent in this analysis. Thus the comments of the TG and LLE groups were unfavourable in 43 percent and 40 percent of cases respectively, compared with only 30 percent for the RW group. Table 7.6 presents a tabulation of the most common comments, as expressed by students in each group. Where synonymous descriptions were used, the figures were combined with those of the most frequently used comment. The figures represent percentages of all comments made by pupils within each group.

Table 7.6

Comments on English as Expressed by Fifth Form Students Taking 3 English Courses

Percentage of Comments

Comment	TG %	RW %	LLE %
Interesting	16.1	14.3	6.7
Useful	11.1	14.3	8.3
Variety	7.4	8.6	3.3
Easy	8.6	8.6	8.3
Imaginative	8.6	5.7	11.7
Boring	21.0	12.9	15.0
Repetitive	12.4	4.3	3.3
Useless	12.4	2.8	3.3
Difficult	8.6	7.1	5.0

No significance tests were applied in view of the subjectivity of the data, but the indications are that the TG pupils found English more 'repetitive', 'boring', and 'useless' than the other groups, whereas the LLE pupils saw it as less 'interesting' or 'useful'.

(b)   *Part 2: Attitudes to English as shown by the Semantic Differential*

Five major topics in English were rated by the pupils using 14 bi-polar adjectival scales, following the principles of the Semantic Differential procedure.[1]

The concepts to be rated were 'Writing Essays', 'Literature', 'Reading'. 'Our Textbook for Language and Composition' and 'Sentence Study'. Each pupil rated every concept on a 7-point scale for each dimension. The mean results for each programme as portrayed in Figure 7.3 were tested for differences by means of conventional t tests. The main trends and differences significant beyond the 0.05 level are listed and interpreted below.

1. C. Osgood, G. Suci and P. Tannenbaum, *The Measurement of Meaning, op. cit.*

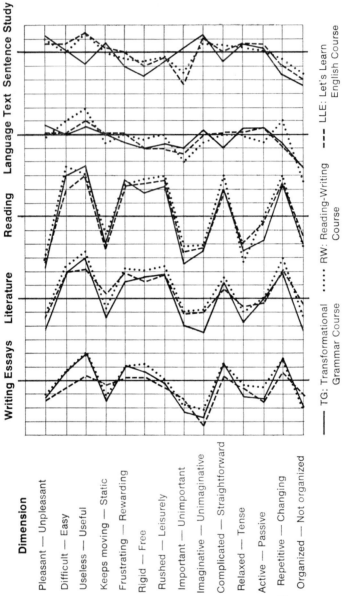

Figure 7.3 *Attitudes to Topics in English as Rated on the Semantic Differential*

(i)   WRITING ESSAYS

In each group essay writing was seen in predominantly positive terms, as 'pleasant', 'useful', 'changing', 'straightforward', 'imaginative', and 'important'. More specifically, the two Oregon groups found it 'easier' and more 'useful' than the LLE pupils. In addition the RW group found it more 'free' than the LLE group, while the TG group rated it as more 'straightforward'. Clearly the LLE group finished their course with less positive attitudes towards essay writing.

(ii)   LITERATURE

The general attitudes revealed towards literature were, like those for essay writing, mostly very favourable. Extreme views were expressed on the dimensions 'pleasant', 'imaginative', 'important', 'organized', 'keeps moving', 'changing', 'useful', 'easy', 'leisurely', and 'rewarding'. In fact, all means were on the positive side of the scale for all dimensions. All the significant differences favoured the Oregon groups, thus reflecting the popularity of the Oregon Literature programme. Both Oregon groups rated literature as more 'useful' than the LLE groups. The TG pupils found it significantly more 'pleasant' and 'straightforward' than the LLE groups, while the RW groups rated it more highly on the 'keeps moving' dimension.

(iii)   READING

Once again, all groups expressed consistently positive attitudes towards reading, especially on the dimensions—'pleasant', 'important', 'relaxed', 'imaginative', 'useful', 'easy', 'rewarding', 'leisurely' and 'free'. No mean score occurred on the negative side of any scale. Three significant differences occurred, all favouring the RW group over the LLE pupils. The former found reading 'easier', more 'relaxed', and more 'straightforward'. It should be noted that throughout the experiment the RW groups more often chose their reading materials themselves, while the LLE groups had it chosen for them.

(iv)   OUR TEXTBOOKS IN LANGUAGE AND COMPOSITION

Nearly all attitudes expressed towards the language and composition textbooks were neutral. In fact, only one dimension drew an extreme position from all groups. All felt that their textbook was 'organized'. Between programmes, however, significant differences occurred on six dimensions. The TG pupils, who were rating the whole of their language text, found it more 'useless', 'unimaginative', 'repetitive', 'passive', 'complicated' and 'unpleasant' than the RW groups, who were rating only the rhetoric section. Clearly, the Transformational Grammar section of the Oregon Curriculum is not liked. The LLE pupils also found their text more 'passive' and 'repetitive' than the RW pupils, but less 'complicated' than the TG pupils.

(v) SENTENCE STUDY

A similar neutrality was found in the rating of the study of sentences. The only adjectives for which extreme positions were taken by most pupils were 'organized' and 'rigid'. Significant differences appeared between programmes, however, on the dimensions expressing usefulness, importance and straightforwardness. The TG groups found sentence analysis 'useless', 'unimportant' and 'complicated'; the other two groups rated it positively on all these qualities. Once again, there is evidence that the TG strand of the Oregon Curriculum is not appreciated by the pupils.

Overall, the Semantic Differential provided a number of illuminating findings which were not picked up in the open-ended questions, or the ranking of subjects. It was easy to administer, and lent itself more readily to statistical analysis than did the open-ended questions.

(c)   *Part 3: Attitude towards Own Progress*

In this section pupils were asked to rate their own progress during the fifth form on aspects of English. The mean scores all fell between 2.15 and 3.08, indicating that all groups felt that there had been moderate improvement in all the aspects examined, but no significant differences occurred between the pupils taking the three courses.

(d)   *Part 4: Attitudes towards Various Activities in English*

As in the fourth form questionnaire, pupils were asked to rate on a 5-point scale the extent to which they liked or disliked 10 different activities connected with writing, reading, discussion, etc. As Figure 7.4 shows, the mean scores extended from 1.39 to 3.23, indicating a range of attitudes in this section. The most positive ratings were expressed for reading fiction and writing imaginative stories; the most negative for sentence study, writing to persuade, and play-reading in class. The between-course comparisons showed only 3 significant differences out of a possible 30, and all occurred at the 0.05 level. Contrary to expectation, the RW group liked imaginative writing significantly less than the TG or LLE groups ($t=2.50$ and 2.49 respectively). In the only other finding to reach the criterion of significance, the LLE pupils expressed a stronger liking for reading non-fiction than did the TG group ($t=2.03$). As these findings were not supported in the third and fourth form questionnaires, and as they barely reached the criterion of significance, they may be best viewed as chance differences. Unlike the Semantic Differential scale, the straightforward like-dislike questionnaire was unable to detect differences in attitudes expressed by the three groups towards their English studies.

SIXTH FORM FOLLOW-UP

At the end of their sixth-form year, only 57 of the original pupils were still at school, and available for a follow-up assessment. All had been

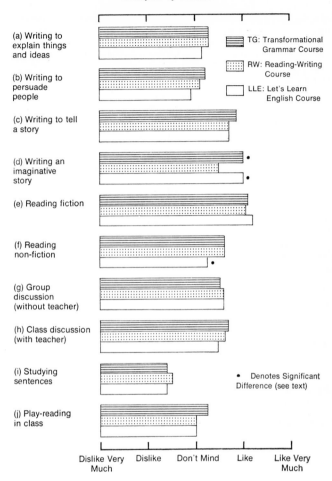

Figure 7.4 *Attitudes to English—Form 4*

taking a common sixth form English programme, with a major emphasis on literature, composition, and socio-linguistics, and minimal work on formal language. Nevertheless, it was felt that a follow-up study might be profitable, if it could throw more light on the suspected differences found at the fifth form level. As no differences had emerged between programmes on the main writing criteria throughout the experiment, and as there was a hint that the Oregon pupils had acquired a greater control over sentence structure, it was decided to attempt an exercise in which

F

they might apply such skills in a different writing exercise, namely précis writing.

In the course of the analysis the pupils in the TG group were found to be slightly superior on the matching ability tests used in Form 3, therefore three of their brighter pupils were dropped from the sixth form sample. Table 7.7 sets out the précis results, for the three groups, as marked by the independent panel of English teachers on the three criteria, mechanics, style and content. Once again, the three groups were extraordinarily similar in their performance, thus confirming the earlier finding that the different programmes had produced no important differential effects on the pupils.

Table 7.7

Means and Standard Deviations for Précis Writing—End of Form 6

	TG				RW				LLE			
N	16				20				18			
Variable	Mech.	Style	Cont.	Total	Mech.	Style	Cont.	Total	Mech.	Style	Cont.	Total
Mean	7.38	7.25	8.13	22.76	8.00	7.55	7.85	23.40	7.83	7.33	8.17	23.33
SD	2.80	2.59	2.29	7.14	2.30	2.40	1.82	5.76	2.59	2.11	2.09	6.03

Summary of Main Results

The major purpose of the investigation was to identify any divergent effects on the language growth of secondary school pupils as a result of studying three different English programmes over a period of three years. The results presented in this chapter show clearly that these divergencies are surprisingly small in both writing and reading skills. Certain patterns of attitudinal differences did emerge, but even these differences are by no means striking.

A summary of the main comparative findings is outlined below.

(1) *Form Three*

(a) At the end of one year there were no identifiable differences resulting from the three programmes on any *writing* criteria, in *reading comprehension* or *vocabulary*, in *formal language* measures, or in *literary appreciation*. Similarly there were no differences attributable to the teachers, regardless of programme.

(b) The TG pupils showed less favourable attitudes towards *reading* and *writing* after one year, but on all other attitudinal scales no significant differences appeared between programmes.

(2) *Form Four*

(a) After two years, there were still no measurable differences in any *writing, reading, literature* or *formal language* skills amongst the three programme groups, and only minor differences attributable to the teachers.

(b) The pupils studying the Oregon materials showed a stronger liking for literature and for explanatory and persuasive writing than the LLE groups. The TG pupils also felt that they were writing more clearly, but revealed less confidence in their progress in English in other respects.

(3) *Form Five*

(a) After three years, some statistically significant differences in test scores did appear. The pupils taking the Oregon course, with and without transformational grammar, showed somewhat greater skill in *sentence combining* exercises, while the two grammar groups performed slightly better on the conventions of *English usage*, but not specifically on their understanding of what constitutes a sentence. No differences were found between programmes on *essay writing, reading* or *literature*, nor on the three-hour *School Certificate English* examination.

(b) Several differences in attitudes were identified by means of the semantic differential method. Both Oregon groups enjoyed *writing* and *literature* more than the LLE group, while the RW pupils also showed greater enthusiasm for *reading*. The TG pupils were noticeably discontented with their *language textbooks* and with their sentence analysis studies, which they described as 'complicated', 'useless', and 'unimportant'. These conclusions were confirmed in their open-ended comments.

(4) *Form Six Follow-up*

One year after the completion of the study, there were still no observable differences between the groups in their writing skills, as assessed by a *précis writing* test.

(5) *Conclusion*

From these findings, it is difficult to escape the conclusion that English grammar, whether traditional or transformational, has virtually no effect on the language growth of typical high school students. This conclusion applies to courses in transformational grammar, as taught in the Oregon Curriculum, and in the traditional grammar contained in the LLE series. In short, the RW pupils survived three years of schooling without any kind of formal grammar study, yet they performed just as well at the end of their fifth form year on all conventional measures of writing and reading. The transformational grammar groups may have gained a slight advantage in exercises deliberately testing minor conventions of usage, and the combining of sentences (without using 'and'), but such competencies, if real, were not reflected in their actual writing performance. Moreover, this slight advantage was gained at the cost of a negative attitude towards formal language work. Scarcely any pupil completed the course with a favourable attitude towards grammar or its value.

8

Further Analyses of Writing Quality

In the previous chapter it was shown that on no conventional measures of language growth did the grammar and non-grammar students reveal any important differences. It is possible, however, that the effects of grammar are more subtle, that they influence a student's writing style in ways not readily identified by conventional measures. Perhaps the grammar students were using a wider range of transformations, joining their sentences differently, making greater use of subordination or a wider vocabulary.

As the conditions of this investigation were regarded as unique, and the data difficult to collect a second time, it was decided to pursue these suppositions as far as possible, by making a more penetrating examination of the essays written by the three groups. These investigations are described below.

Analysis of T-Units

One method of studying a student's writing style is to examine the length of his sentences. It has often been found that mature writers use longer sentences, made up of more subordinate clauses, phrases, and numerous other linguistic structures. It is a plausible hypothesis that a study of grammar might lead students to produce a greater number of such long, complex sentences. Unfortunately it has been found that the relationship between writing ability and sentence length is confused by the tendency of many immature writers to construct long sentences by stringing together series of kernel sentences with the conjunctions 'and' and 'so'. Hunt[1] has

1. K. W. Hunt, *Grammatical Structures Written at Three Grade Levels*, Research Report No. 3 (Urbana, Illinois: NCTE, 1965).

therefore suggested, and many researchers have since adopted, the use of the T-unit as the basic unit for examining this relationship. A T-unit is an abbreviation for a 'minimal terminable unit', and by Hunt's definition includes 'one main clause plus all the subordinate clauses attached to or embedded within it'. In his research, he found that mature writers tend to write in longer T-units, and, in particular, to use adjectival clauses more frequently. Thus, American 4th and 8th grade pupils were found to write T-units only 60 percent and 80 percent as long as those of 12th graders. The corresponding figures for adjectival clauses were 46 percent and 68 percent respectively. The differences between these grade levels on the criterion of sentence length were much less—79 percent and 94 percent respectively.

In line with such findings, it was decided to examine T-units, subordinate clauses, and other transformations in the writing undertaken by the students in the present project. To test the hypothesis that a study of grammar would induce students to write in longer T-units, a representative sample of 58 essays was drawn from all those written in the fifth form by the students in each of the three programmes. The sample of essays chosen was representative of each group, but not of all the essays written, as a disproportionately large number was deliberately chosen from Topic D, the question used in both the third and fifth forms. This meant that over one third of the essays chosen for analysis were written on the topic 'He saw the gap and decided it was now or never . . .' The selection of Topic D essays facilitated a subsequent analysis, and the students' choice of 'The Gap' reflected the popularity of this topic.

A check on the equivalence of the students chosen for this study was made by examining their total fifth form essay marks. This revealed a very close similarity between groups. The respective means for the TG, RW and LLE groups on the Essay Total were 79.3, 76.2 and 78.5 respectively. The standard deviations were all close to 15; therefore, it was concluded that the differences in mean scores were negligible, and the groups adequately matched for the purpose of the analysis.

To prevent any possible bias in the identification and counting of T-units, the essays from each group were mixed together, and, as they were not marked by pupil name or programme, it was not possible to tell which essay belonged to which group. The first 10 T-units in each essay were identified, and the total number of words in these 10 units counted for each essay. A preliminary analysis had shown that most essays contained between 10 and 20 T-units, but in order to ensure that no particular pupils produced a disproportionately large influence on the results, it was decided that the number of T-units analysed for each essay should be uniform. The segmentation of sentences into T-units followed the principles outlined by Hunt, with minor modifications based on Mellon.[2] Thus:

(1) Each independent clause, plus its subordinate clauses and embeddings counted as one T-unit.

2. J. C. Mellon, *op. cit.*

(2) The coordinating conjunctions 'and', 'but', 'yet', 'or', and 'so' (when it meant 'and so') were regarded as markers which separate adjacent T-units (except in cases where they separated two subordinate clauses).

(3) A clause was defined as an expression which contained a subject (or coordinated subjects) and a finite verb (or coordinated finite verbs).

(4) Sentence fragments which resulted from the omission of a single word were counted as T-units, with the missing word supplied.

(5) Interjections, parentheses, unintelligible words, vocatives and speaker tags in conversation were discarded.

Examples

(1) The policeman tracked down the thief. (1 T-unit)
(2) The policeman and the dog hunted and tracked down the thief. (1 T-unit)
(3) The policeman hunted through the thick bushes/and tracked down the thief. (2 T-units)
(4) The policeman, with his dog, hunted all night for the thief who had stolen and abandoned the new car/but did not catch him. (2 T-units)

Table 8.1 sets out the results of the analysis of words, calculated per T-unit. As it was possible that the narrative essays written on 'The Gap' might have produced different results from the remaining essays, which were largely expository, the figures were examined separately. Overall, 1,740 T-units were included in this analysis.

Table 8.1

Mean Number of Words per T-Unit Written by Students in 3 English Programmes—End of Form 5

Essay	TG			RW			LLE		
	N	M	SD	N	M	SD	N	M	SD
'The Gap'	21	12.7	2.6	19	13.8	4.2	28	12.9	3.6
Remainder	37	12.9	3.5	39	13.3	4.0	30	14.6	4.3
Total	58	12.8	3.2	58	13.5	4.1	58	14.0	4.1

Once again, it is plain that there are no significant differences between groups. Neither grammar group could be said to be writing in longer T-units than the RW students, and no significant differences were found between the different essay topics.

Number of Transformations

In Chapter 2 it was shown that earlier evaluations of courses in transformational grammar had produced some support for the belief that pupils
who are exposed to such a programme may use greater numbers of certain
kinds of transformations in their writing. To investigate this hypothesis,
the 174 essays used in the analysis of T-unit length were subjected to an
intensive examination of the transformations used in these T-units.

For the purposes of this analysis the following transformations were
counted. They were included because they had been studied in the Oregon
TG course.

1. Prepositional phrases
2. Subordinate clauses
3. Adjectives preceding their nouns
4. Participles
5. Gerunds
6. Possessives
7. Absolutes
8. Passives
9. Appositives
10. Comparatives
11. Adverbs
12. Deletions

As in the previous analysis, the anonymity of the pupils was retained,
and essays from each group mixed together, to safeguard against possible
bias.

Table 8.2 sets out, for the sample of essays from each group, the mean
number of transformations in the first 10 T-units. Table 8.3 presents comparable figures on the mean number of transformations per 10 words of
writing.

Each table shows that no differences emerged in the number of transformations used by the pupils taking the three different programmes.
Apparently, the students' study of transformations in the TG course did

Table 8.2

*Mean Number of Transformations per 10 T-Units for Essays Written
in 3 English Programmes*

Essay	N	TG M	SD	N	RW M	SD	N	LLE M	SD
'The Gap'	21	34.1	10.9	19	35.2	14.0	28	31.8	12.5
Remainder	37	35.2	12.0	39	35.1	13.4	30	37.1	13.0
Total	58	34.6	11.3	58	35.1	13.5	58	34.6	12.7

Table 8.3

*Mean Number of Transformations per 10 Words for Essays
Written in 3 English Programmes*

Essay	N	TG M	SD	N	RW M	SD	N	LLE M	SD
'The Gap'	21	2.6	0.5	19	2.6	0.4	28	2.4	0.4
Remainder	37	2.6	0.5	39	2.8	0.5	30	2.7	0.9
Total	58	2.6	0.5	58	2.8	0.5	58	2.6	0.7

not produce any tendency to use them with greater frequency in their writing.

To explore the possibility of more subtle stylistic differences, a further investigation was undertaken to determine whether the pattern of transformations used was different for each group. For the 58 essays in each group, each of the 12 kinds of transformations was compared separately and the results are presented in Table 8.4.

As in previous analyses, the most noticeable feature of Table 8.4 is the remarkable similarity in the pattern of mean scores across the three programmes. The only difference of any magnitude in the 36 possible contrasts occurred in the case of participles, where t tests showed that the

Table 8.4

*Mean Number of Specific Transformations per 10 T-Units
for Essays Written in 3 English Programmes
(N=58 in Each Group)*

Transformation	TG M	SD	RW M	SD	LLE M	SD
Prep. Phrases	12.20	5.04	11.43	5.21	10.80	4.62
Sub. Clauses	5.67	3.34	5.41	3.42	4.97	3.32
Adjectives	6.54	4.56	7.62	5.24	7.51	4.45
Participles	1.33	1.10	2.10	2.24	2.40	2.90
Gerunds	0.24	0.57	0.41	0.72	0.38	0.85
Possessives	0.36	0.66	0.48	0.92	0.47	0.75
Absolutes	0.19	0.54	0.22	0.53	0.16	0.36
Passives	1.34	1.99	1.21	1.75	1.78	1.80
Appositives	0.91	1.22	0.62	0.89	0.57	0.83
Comparatives	0.31	0.59	0.36	0.81	0.48	0.77
Adverbs	3.76	2.41	3.33	2.22	3.76	2.63
Deletions	1.29	1.85	1.64	2.06	1.16	1.28
Total	34.59	11.27	35.14	13.50	34.61	12.67

TG group used significantly fewer than the RW and LLE groups (t=2.30, p<0.05 and t=2.62, p<0.01). There is no support in these figures for the hypothesis that a special study of any kind of transformation increases the propensity to use them.

Additional findings about the relationships between these various indices are of interest. In each group the number of words per T-unit correlated highly with the total number of transformations per T-unit (r=0.86, 0.88 and 0.70 for the TG, RW and LLE groups respectively). As the former index is considerably easier to calculate, this finding is of some practical value. However, these indices seem to bear little relationship to conventional measures of quality.

The correlation coefficients for each group between the total fifth form essay mark and the number of transformations per 10 words were 0.10, 0.22 and - 0.07 for the TG, RW and LLE groups respectively. Thus, it seems doubtful whether this kind of analysis makes any important contribution to the assessment of quality in writing, as it is traditionally assessed.

Breadth of Vocabulary

It is a plausible assumption that pupils who spend more of their time reading and writing would extend their vocabularies at a greater rate than those who devote more time to grammar studies. Such a hypothesis was not supported by the results obtained from the vocabulary tests at any age level. Nevertheless, it is possible that greater breadth of vocabulary might be shown in the students' essay writing.

To investigate this possibility, a random sample of 170 essays was identified, drawn from all three groups. For the first 100 words in each essay, a count was made of the number of words not included in the NZCER Alphabetical Spelling List. As this list is made up of the most common 2,700 words used by New Zealand children in their essays, it was felt to be a sensitive guide for identifying the proportion of infrequently used words. In fact, it revealed wide individual differences amongst pupils, ranging from 0 to 19 'rare' words per 100 words, with an overall mean of 7.0.

After analysis, the essays were divided into three groups, according to the respective English programmes taken by the students who wrote them, and the mean number of rare words was calculated for each group. Table 8.5 shows that, once again, there were no differences between groups. The largest inter-programme t value was only 1.84. If the RW children were introduced to a wider range of words, it was not reflected in their essay writing.

Amount of Growth in Writing Skill

The lack of differential effects of the programmes on writing performance gave rise to a further question. How much growth did occur in writing

Table 8.5

*Mean Number of 'Rare' Words Used
in Essays Written in 3 English
Programmes*

	TG	RW	LLE
M	6.70	6.12	7.47
SD	3.98	3.31	4.41

skill during the course of the experiment? Clearly, if there were little change in ability during the high school years, it would be unlikely that any particular English programme could demonstrate superiority over others in promoting change.

To explore this matter, the essays of all pupils who had written on the same topic in 1970 and 1972 were compared. As outlined in Chapter 6, the essays for both class levels were marked together in such a way that the teachers were unaware which essays had been written in the third form and which in the fifth form. After marking, the essays were re-sorted into class levels, and the marks analysed.

The average gain for the 141 pupils, over the two-year period, did appear to be surprisingly small. The mean score for the third-form essays was 18.06 out of a possible 32. For the fifth form essays the corresponding figure was 20.98, representing a gain of 2.92 marks over two years. This figure is equivalent to 60 percent of the standard deviation of the third form essay marks. It was a statistically significant gain ($t = 6.21$), but by no means reassuring. In percentage terms, the mean score of these pupils increased from 56.4 percent to 65.6 percent.

Further examination reveals, however, that much of the explanation for the disappointing growth is attributable to the unreliability of gain scores in the measurement of writing skill. To investigate this problem, a check was made on the extent of agreement between markers. For these essays the correlation between the marks given by pairs of independent markers was found to be 0.64. As the marks were pooled for pairs of markers, the marker reliability of the marks actually analysed was estimated at 0.78. Thus the error variance due to markers would be approximately 22 percent. However, variability of pupil performance would increase the error variance by at least an equivalent amount (see Chapter 10), producing a reliability coefficient of approximately 0.56. Furthermore, the correlation between third and fifth form essay marks was found to be 0.48, which is high, relative to the estimated reliability. Thus, the reliability of gain scores in this analysis would be estimated at somewhere between 0.15 and 0.20, which is barely significant at the 0.05 level.[2] Under these circum-

2. The formula used for calculating the reliability of difference scores was:

$$r_{\text{diff}_{12}} = \frac{\frac{r_{11} + r_{22}}{2} - r_{12}}{1 - r_{12}}$$

stances it is not surprising that the measured gain appears to be small. In fact, Diederich[3] has analysed a number of research studies where growth in language was assessed, and concluded that the gain scores obtained from comparing two single essays are usually so unreliable that this strategy is best avoided where possible. It was on this advice that the present study was designed in such a way as to match the three groups initially, and thus avoid the analysis of gain scores.

Nevertheless, on the question of how much growth actually occurred in essay writing skills, it is impossible to draw precise conclusions. Suffice it to say that the gain, as measured, was significant. Furthermore, the reliability coefficient obtained from the pooled marks of the four essays written at the end of the fifth form (at least 0.80) was considerably higher than that of the gain scores calculated from single essays (below 0.20). In other words, if one English programme had been clearly superior in promoting growth in writing skills, it should have been able to demonstrate its advantage when the total scores based on four essays were analysed.

Summary

In Chapter 7 it was shown that there were no important differences in the effects of the three English programmes, after three years, in the quality of writing they produced, as judged by the traditional criteria of content, style, organization and mechanics. These findings were confirmed by the objective analyses described above in Chapter 8.

None of the groups was found to be superior to the others in:

(1) The length of T-units used in their essays.
(2) The number of transformations per T-unit.
(3) The number of transformations per 10 words.
(4) The pattern of transformations used.
(5) The breadth of the vocabulary used.

Clearly, the learning of grammar, either transformational or traditional, has little impact on a student's essay writing.

3. P. B. Diederich, 'Problems and Possibilities of Research in the Teaching of Written Composition', in *Research Design in the Teaching of English*, ed. D. H. Russell et al. (Champaign, Illinois: NCTE, 1964).

9

Teachers' Evaluation of the Courses

One important approach to the evaluation of any course is to seek the opinions of teachers who have taught it. This information was obtained for the Oregon Curriculum and LLE courses by two methods.

Firstly, an objective questionnaire was sent to all teachers known to the investigators who had had the experience of teaching both courses. Fifteen teachers, all teaching in large Auckland secondary schools, provided their opinions on a comparison of the content, organization and interest value of the two courses. The results of this analysis are set out below in Table 9.1.

Further information was obtained on more specific aspects of the courses from the three teachers who participated in the investigation. Their reactions are also summarized below. It should be noted that in both cases the teachers made their comments without the benefit of information about the outcome of the experiment.

Table 9.1 presents the results of the analysis of the opinions of the 15 teachers on those aspects of the courses detailed in the questionnaire. Teachers were asked to rate each section of both courses on seven criteria, on a three-point scale—'very good', 'good', and 'unsuitable'. The overall pattern indicates that the Oregon Curriculum is more highly regarded on nearly all criteria. Teachers who have used both courses believe that the Oregon Curriculum has more appropriate aims, is better organized, provides more suitable exercises, is more interesting for students, and offers the teacher considerably more intellectual satisfaction. For all these criteria the differences in opinions between the two courses were significant at the 0.01 level. On the criteria of reading difficulty and variety of approach the differences in ratings were negligible. The results of the χ^2 tests used to examine the differences between the two courses are presented at the right hand side of the table.

Table 9.1
Teachers' Evaluation of the Courses

Criterion	Rating	Oregon Curriculum				'Let's Learn English' Series					χ^2	Significance of Difference
		Language	Rhetoric	Literature	Total	Language	Reading	Writing	Speaking & Listening	Total		
1. Appropriate aims	V. Good	2	10	13	25	4	6	5	2	17	15.27	0.01
	Good	3	–	–	3	2	3	4	5	14		
	Unsuitable	–	–	–	0	4	2	2	1	9		
2. Organization sequence	V. Good	5	8	12	25	–	2	3	1	6	36.64	0.01
	Good	–	2	1	3	4	7	4	4	19		
	Unsuitable	–	–	–	0	6	2	4	3	15		
3. Variety of approach	V. Good	–	3	4	7	1	2	2	3	8	0.02	NS
	Good	4	6	8	18	4	5	7	4	20		
	Unsuitable	1	1	1	3	6	4	2	1	13		
4. Suitable exercises	V. Good	4	4	5	13	1	4	4	3	10	6.92	0.01
	Good	–	6	7	13	2	5	5	3	16		
	Unsuitable	–	–	1	1	6	1	1	1	10		
5. Reading difficulty level	V. Good	1	4	4	9	2	5	5	4	14	0.12	NS
	Good	2	4	7	13	6	4	4	2	17		
	Unsuitable	1	1	2	4	2	1	1	1	5		
6. Interest for students	V. Good	–	4	11	15	1	4	4	2	9	8.34	0.01
	Good	3	6	2	11	6	6	6	4	22		
	Unsuitable	2	–	1	2	4	3	1	2	10		
7. Intellectually satisfying for teacher	V. Good	4	9	13	26	1	1	2	1	5	42.88	0.01
	Good	1	1	–	2	4	5	2	4	15		
	Unsuitable	–	–	–	0	5	5	7	3	20		

All but two of these teachers had taught both courses for three years or more. They therefore had had ample opportunity to identify particular weaknesses and strengths. Some of these were incorporated in the teachers' comments made at the end of the questionnaire. Some felt that the Oregon Curriculum is scholarly and more appropriate for brighter children, and is correspondingly difficult for slower pupils. Only one teacher commented on the American emphasis. Most felt the Curriculum succeeded in achieving an obvious sense of direction. Students could see some evidence of progress.

Comments on Smart's texts were less favourable, but several teachers saw it as a useful supplement to the Oregon Curriculum, particularly for slower pupils. It appears to provide a comprehensive range of exercises, designed to fulfil many needs as the occasion arises. As a source book, some teachers found it 'highly acceptable where the primary teaching aims are experience-/or interest-centred, rather than intellectual'.

COMMENTS OF THE TEACHERS INVOLVED IN THE RESEARCH STUDY

The Oregon Curriculum

(a) *General Comments*

The three teachers directly involved in the research agreed that they found the Oregon course a satisfying one to teach. Amongst the advantages cited were the consistent emphasis on basic concepts, which gave teachers confidence that all activities were related to the essential nature of the subject. The structure of the strands building, as they do, on what goes before, and leading, in turn, to future activities, gave teachers a sense of progress and achievement which they felt was shared by their classes. The material was generally felt to be well organized for an inductive approach to learning, a process which led to a great deal of class discussion. The teachers felt relieved from the burden of providing all the necessary materials for an English course themselves, a course which might well reflect their own inadequacies as much as their strengths.

The three teachers were somewhat surprised at their own reaction in this respect. They had previously shared the commonly held view that the English teacher must have freedom to create his own course, culling from a wide variety of sources. From the outset they feared that such a structured course would become a straight-jacket. But the Oregon Curriculum was found to have, within its structure, a great deal of room for teachers to express their own personalities and emphases. All teachers felt that they had confidence in most of the teaching material, and yet they had sufficient freedom to handle it in their own way, thus producing something distinctly better than they would have without the Oregon Curriculum.

The teachers found that the Oregon Curriculum required just as much preparation as did teaching in their own way; a great deal of work had to be done to prepare for the presentation of the material so that it could be taught in a variety of ways appropriate to their classes. But the time spent appeared to be more productive than would have been the case if it had been spent mainly in a search for material.

(b)   *The Literature Strand*

This strand makes good use of the notion of the spiral. The basic concepts of *subject, form* and *point of view* were well chosen in that they could be grasped readily by third formers in a simple form while lending themselves to more complex development as the course progressed. While there was emphasis on the whole work, and the enjoyment of it as good literature, students seemed able also to reach a deeper understanding through consideration of the basic concepts. For instance, both RW and LLE groups read Steinbeck's *The Red Pony* in the third form, and the teachers of the LLE classes believed that these classes did not attain the same depth of understanding as that gained by the RW classes, who could apply their knowledge of the Oregon Curriculum *Literature* concepts.

One aspect of the course that was questioned by the teachers is the emphasis on 'reservoir literature' in the book used in the fourth form, *Literature III*. Here *Arthurian Legends* and *The Odyssey* are included, not to develop concepts but as part of the cultural heritage of English speaking people. But, of course, teachers were free to use this section selectively, and in a way appropriate to their students. For New Zealand pupils, a significant lack is the absence of works such as Maori and Polynesian myths and legends.

A further problem developed as the years progressed. Teachers found that the slower students in the classes experienced some difficulty with the sophisticated literary passages studied. This was most marked in Form 5. The inclusion of more passages with a lower level of reading difficulty would help solve this problem.

(c)   *The Rhetoric Strand*

This is the strand most concerned with a utilitarian aim, to improve students' ability to communicate in writing and speaking. The teachers felt that its emphasis on *audience* and *appropriateness* generally resulted in writing that was well directed to a particular goal. The emphasis on appropriateness rather than on correctness did not seem to lead to a lowering of standards, but appeared to bring students to see poor spelling, sentence structure and unconventional punctuation as a barrier to full communication in formal situations. The basic concepts of *substance, structure* and *style* were agreed to be well chosen; they also lend themselves readily to a study of mass media. Here, the influence of purpose and audience on the three basic aspects of communication, was found to be especially clearly illustrated. In the rhetoric strand as a whole the teachers enjoyed concentrating on the essence of communication rather than being caught up largely in surface skills such as punctuation and usage.

Most chapters are arranged in a similar pattern. The students are generally given a passage, which they read and discuss to discover a principle which is then reinforced by short exercises in preparation for the application of the principle in their own writing in an assignment at the end of the chapter. Although the passages and exercises are very well arranged for the inductive process to take place, teachers have to make a special effort to use a variety of approaches to maintain the interest of the students.

The teachers felt that many of the structures encountered were not well remembered. Students discovered techniques and applied them, and then moved on to the next stage. If they are to retain them as part of their repertoire, as it were, more revision and drilling of these principles should be built into the course. In some cases, of course, this might not be desirable, as it would be enough to discover the wide range of substances, structures and styles appropriate in different situations and purposes for students to become more sensitive to the demands of the language situations in which they find themselves, and to search harder than before for appropriate language.

(d) *The Language Strand*

Only the TG group studied this strand, which is largely made up of transformational grammar.

The teachers found this particular system of grammar was well-structured and intellectually satisfying to them. They felt that students in the TG classes gained an insight into their language which they would not normally have. Students' interest was generally sustained for much of the first two years of the course, and many students were fascinated by the new insights gained.

The basic concepts underlying the course were developed after discovering the phrase structure rules and examining two or three transformations. Students quickly grasped the idea that they have an inbuilt knowledge of basic sentence structures and that relatively few transformation rules, applied again and again, allow them to generate an infinite number of sentences. Having reached this point, teachers found that some members of the classes did not enjoy studying more transformations which were merely further illustrations of a concept already understood.

At the beginning of Form 5, the classes had a long period of revision. This section is included in the course at this point in order to cater for American students who might be using the Oregon Curriculum for the first time when they entered senior High School. The thoroughness of the revision is illustrated by the fact that some students who arrived in the TG classes at the beginning of Form 5 learned the grammar as successfully as those who had begun at Form 3. In retrospect, teachers of the classes felt that they should have by-passed this revision and kept on with new

G

work; interest tended to flag at this point and was difficult to regain. Pressure of examinations on the students and their feeling that grammar was not directly related to examination work might well have aggravated this tendency. Nevertheless the teachers felt that the whole TG course might be shortened with profit, provided that it did not result in an increase of didactic teaching.

Reading and Writing in the RW Course

The RW group followed this programme instead of learning grammar. The teachers felt that this was a profitable course on the whole. Most students appeared to enjoy the additional wide reading involved and to benefit from it. The creative writing done by students was relished by a few members of the class more than the others. Once the students settled into the routine of reading silently, both students and teachers enjoyed the change of activity. Teachers found that they needed to be familiar with the books students enjoy in order to help ensure that all of the class had a suitable book. Although most members of the classes were happy to read, there was a handful of students in each class who did not settle readily and who had to be supervised carefully. Generally speaking, teachers found that students read more intently in the classroom than they did in the library.

A feeling that this work lacked direction was the most serious criticism made of it, although teachers realized that this was a feature inherent in the nature of the course.

The LLE Course

This course consisted primarily of formal work from the source text book series *Let's Learn English* by P. R. Smart. This was supplemented with literary works selected from the resources of the teacher and the school.

The teachers recognized the merits of the author, who laboured single-handed in assembling this series. There was much evidence of imagination and consideration of the interests of the students in selecting material for inclusion. In comparison with other courses they had encountered over a number of years, however, the teachers found it unsatisfactory in certain aspects.

Its overriding weakness, they felt, was lack of direction. Teachers missed both the unity provided by repeated reference to basic concepts, and the sense of progress provided by their development. There is no underlying structure in *Let's Learn English*—the teacher selects the material he requires. And yet in some parts of the book, in the Language section of *Let's Learn English in the 70's*, for example, there is some sequence of skills or ideas to be developed. Teachers found this section rather a mixture of ideas, and in many cases here, and in other parts of the books where material was provided for inductive learning steps in the process of discovery, the exercises were not carefully graded.

The *Speaking* and *Listening* section was found to be rather vague and not very helpful. The teachers found work in Literature rather sketchy and somewhat out of place in a book of this sort. They felt that the attempt to improve reading skill and speed was laudable, but found the exercises difficult to handle in class. The strongest point of the series in the opinion of the teachers lay in the work on the mass media, which was relevant and interesting for the students. Generally, teachers felt that there was little evidence of growth in perception or skill, as a result of the LLE course, beyond that provided by the students' natural growth and maturity.

Conclusion

On the whole, the teachers' attitudes to the Oregon Curriculum were consistent with those of the students. The Literature and Rhetoric sections were regarded favourably by both groups, but the Grammar strand was felt to be unnecessarily long and repetitive. While the Curriculum as a whole provided more intellectual challenge, it was generally felt to be less suitable for the slower pupils.

By contrast, the teachers saw significantly less value in the LLE course than the students did. What the teachers saw as weaknesses in lack of direction and insufficient grading of exercises were apparently not identified as such by the students. Their overall rating of the series was rather neutral, neither good nor bad.

10

Reliability of Essay Marking

The elaborate multiple-marking procedures adopted in this investigation for assessing the essays written by the students in three English programmes provided an ideal opportunity to study the reliability of essay marking. In many ways, the situation resembled a typical marking session in an external examination in English. A panel of experienced English teachers was selected; they were briefed carefully on the criteria and marking patterns to be adopted; they marked and discussed 'guinea-pig' scripts; then they worked systematically through several hundred essays, marking according to the criteria discussed. Thus, it is reasonable to conclude that the reliability of the procedures adopted in this study would throw light on the reliability of essay marking in secondary school external examinations.

In the Form 3 evaluation programme, each pupil in the experiment wrote four essays, each of which was assessed by four different English teachers, according to the criteria on which they had agreed in the briefing session—content, organization, style and mechanics. As each teacher marked out of a total of 16 marks for each pupil, and each essay was marked four times, the total possible mark for each essay was 16 x 4, or 64 marks. And as each pupil had written four essays the total possible mark for each pupil was 64 x 4, or 256.

Three related analyses were undertaken with the Form 3 essay marks.* Firstly, the correlation coefficients between the marks assigned by different markers to the same essays were calculated in order to determine the reliability of the markers. Secondly, an analysis of variance was undertaken to determine how much of the variance in essay marks is

*The authors are indebted to Mr J. H. Darwin, formerly of the Applied Mathematics Laboratory of the Department of Scientific and Industrial Research (DSIR), for his assistance in some of the calculations described in this chapter.

attributable to the markers and how much to the pupils themselves, when they wrote about different topics on different days.

A third analysis was designed to illustrate how much accuracy is lost by using fewer than 16 assessments of the students' writing, and incidentally to determine the optimum number of essays and markers to use when high levels of reliability are essential.

Reliability of Markers

Each of the 16 English teachers marked approximately 60 of the essays on each of the 4 essay topics on which the pupils had written at the end of Form 3. As the essays had been assigned randomly to markers, and as instructions had been given to use all points on the scale with approximately equal emphasis, it would be reasonable to expect a similar range and central tendency in the marks assigned to each teacher. Inspection of the means and standard deviations of these marks, however, showed considerable variation in a few cases.

Thus, for Topic A, the mean of the marks given by one teacher was as high as 11.7 out of 16; for another it was only 9.28; and these were marks given to the same set of essays. The range of marks on all four topics is presented in Table 10.1.

Table 10.1
*Range of Means and Standard Deviations for Essay Marks
Given by Different Markers*

Topic	Highest Mean	Lowest Mean	Highest SD	Lowest SD
A	11.77	9.28	3.00	2.03
B	10.39	9.32	3.20	2.21
C	10.42	8.63	2.83	1.87
D	10.62	8.79	3.37	2.27

Over all topics, approximately two-thirds of the markers produced a mean score between 60 percent and 65 percent in their set of 60 essays, and the discrepancies found between the means of individual markers were virtually eliminated when their marks were combined to produce a grand total for each pupil.

Some variation was found also in the spread of marks assigned by each teacher. Thus, for Topic A the standard deviations ranged from 2.03 to 3.00 out of 16. Comparable variations were found in the other topics, as can be seen in Table 10.1. As other research studies have shown, some teachers cluster their marks around the mean, while others spread them out more widely.

Main attention in this analysis was focussed, however, on the correlations between the marks assigned by teachers to the same essays. How closely did they agree in their assessments of individual essays? Table 10.2 shows the highest, lowest, and median correlation coefficients for pairs of markers on each topic, and the total pattern over all topics. These correlations are based on samples of 60 essays.

Table 10.2

Correlations between Marks Assigned by Individual Teachers to the Same Essays

Topic	Highest r	Lowest r	Median r
A	0.80	0.46	0.62
B	0.81	0.56	0.69
C	0.79	0.44	0.71
D	0.80	0.49	0.67
Median	0.80	0.48	0.68

The median correlation between the assessments made by these markers is only 0.68. Therefore, approximately one-third of the variance in the marks assigned by well-briefed individual teachers to these English essays is error variance. Looked at another way, at this level of reliability, in an examination where 50 percent of pupils were to pass, one would expect 26 percent of the pupils to be passed by one marker but failed by the second marker. Furthermore if the marks were equally reliable, it can be concluded that half of these cases of disagreement (that is, 13 percent) would be misclassified.

When the assessments of two markers are combined, the situation improves somewhat. The pooled marks of pairs of teachers were correlated with those of other pairs, to produce the results presented in Table 10.3.

The median correlation between the pooled results of pairs of markers increased to 0.77, and most were in the 0.75 to 0.80 range. The error variance has been reduced in consequence from 32 percent to 23 percent. Generalizing from the results, we could assume that if English essays were always marked by two teachers, marking independently, and their marks combined, there would be a small but definite improvement in reliability. The percentage of students passed by one pair and failed by another pair would be reduced from approximately 26 percent to 21 percent, and the percentage of real misclassifications from 13 percent to 10.5 percent. By inference, the pooling of three markers' assessments would improve reliability even further, but the extent of such increase cannot be gauged by this approach as there were only four markers

Table 10.3

Correlations between Pooled Marks Assigned by Pairs of Teachers to the Same Essays

Topic	Highest r	Lowest r	Median r
A	0.83	0.69	0.72
B	0.85	0.79	0.81
C	0.83	0.64	0.77
D	0.85	0.66	0.76
Total	0.84	0.68	0.77

assessing each essay. Reasonable estimates of the degree of improvement expected from three or more markers can be obtained by means of an analysis of variance. This is provided in the next section.

Variability of Pupil Performance

Marker inconsistency is not the only source of unreliability in essay marking. Children vary from day to day in their performance at writing, due to such factors as their health, concentration, interest in the topic, knowledge of the topic, and other idiosyncratic factors. The effect of these variables cannot be determined simply by correlating the marks of pupils writing on different occasions. The correlations would be lowered by the unreliability of the markers' assessments.

Therefore an analysis of variance was undertaken to determine what proportion of variance was attributable to the markers as compared with that contributed by the pupils themselves. In other words, the total variance in essay marks was broken down into the variance contributed by the idiosyncracies of the markers and that contributed by variability in the pupils from one essay to another. Other sources of variance were also determined.

From the total group of 250 pupils, the essays of 4 random samples of 25 pupils were chosen for analysis. The 4 samples provided a representative set of the essays marked by each combination of 4 markers. A three-way analysis of variance (4x4x100) was undertaken to compare the effects of markers, essay topics, and pupil differences, and their relevant interactions. As each essay was marked by only 4 of the 16 possible markers, the pupil-by-marker interaction could not be properly assessed. This was not essential to the analysis, however. Main attention was concentrated on the comparison between the variance associated with markers and that associated with essay topics.

Table 10.4

Three-way Analysis of Variance for Markers, Essays and Pupils (N=100)

Source	S.S.	df.	Mean Square	F	E(m.s.)
Between pupils	5,188	96	54.0	6.12**	$16v_p + 4v_{tp} + v$
Between markers	234	12	19.5	2.32*	$100v_m + 25v_{om} + 12v$
Between topics	202	3	67.3	4.50**	$400v_t + 4v_{tp} + 25v_{tm} + v$
Pupils x topics	2,539	288	8.82	3.77**	$4v_{tp} + v$
Markers x topics	302	36	8.39	3.52**	$25v_{tm} + v$
Residual	2,739	1,152	2.38		v
Total	11,204	1,587			

* Significant at 0.05 level   ** Significant at 0.01 level

Table 10.4 shows that all main effects and interactions were significant, although that between markers was significant only at the 0.05 level. To verify these figures, the marks of a second random sample of 100 pupils were subjected to an analysis of variance, producing very similar results. Estimates of the amount of variance associated with each variable were made using the equations in the right-hand column of Table 10.4. The estimates of variance for markers and topics were remarkably small, 0.13 (1.08 percent) and 0.08 (0.67 percent) respectively, indicating that markers varied little amongst themselves in standards, and that the essay topics varied little in difficulty. As expected, the variance associated with pupils was relatively large, 2.82 (23.50 percent) a reflection of substantial individual differences amongst pupils. Main interest focussed, however, on the two interactions. The variance associated with markers by topics was only 0.22 (1.83 percent) suggesting that markers varied little in standard from one topic to th next. The pupil-by-topic interaction, however, showed an unexpectedly large variance of 1.67 (13.92 percent), over seven times as large.

From these figures it would appear that a large source of variability in assessing a student's performance in essay writing skills is the extent to which he varies from one essay topic to the next. Any one indication of writing skill on one topic is likely to be misleading in a large number of cases. When one considers the other sources of variability as well, it can be said that, for a typical pupil, writing on one of the essay topics given, and marked by any one of the 16 markers, one would expect his mark to vary by as much as 2.7 on a scale from 4 to 16 points (that is, 22.50 percent) in two cases out of three. And this result was obtained with carefully briefed markers.

At this point it could be asked how many essays and markers are required to reduce this variability to an acceptable minimum. On the basis of the variance estimates listed above, if one wished to be 95 percent confident of being within one mark of the true average for a typical pupil, it could not even be achieved with four essays and four markers. However, if one were content to be certain that in two cases out of three, the pupils' essay marks were within one point of his true score, the required variance could be obtained with three essays and two markers. Unfortunately, such a combination is rarely found in traditional methods of assessing essay writing skills.

The estimates of variance obtained from this analysis were further used to calculate the expected marker reliability for one essay when the number of markers was increased by n. For pairs of markers, the marker reliability* in the case of one essay, was estimated at 0.76; for three markers it rose to 0.81; for four markers to 0.85, for five markers to 0.88; for six markers to 0.90. Increases beyond that are very small. Remembering that the figure for one marker was only 0.68, it can be seen that there is profit in increasing the number of markers to four or five when only one essay is written. From the earlier analysis, it would seem that more is gained, however, by increasing the number of essays.

Further Correlational Analyses

To supplement the foregoing analysis, another study was made of the number of markers and essays needed in order to obtain a high level of accuracy in drawing conclusions about pupils' writing skills. One hundred pupils were selected at random and the total marks over all 16 assessments for each of these pupils were correlated with the total derived from fewer than 16 assessments (see Figure 10.1). In the first row the totals from 16 assessments (4 essays x 4 markers) were correlated with totals from 12 assessments (4 essays x 3 markers), then 8 assessments (4 x2), and so on. Such comparisons were made in the knowledge that the correlations would be artificially inflated due to overlap brought about by the inclusion of many of the 16 marks (for each pupil) in each total. All are part-whole correlations. More attention should be devoted, then, in interpretation, to the relative rather than the absolute size of the coefficients. Figure 10.1 presents these part-whole correlations between the best criterion (4 markers x 4 essays) and each other combination of markers and essays.

Each reduction was made by dropping the marks contributed by one marker (or one essay) at random. Thus, to obtain the 3 x 4 total for the first pupil, his fourth essay mark was omitted; for the second pupil his third essay mark was omitted, and so on.

---

* The formula for this calculation is given as $r_{11} = \dfrac{v_t + v_p + v_{tp}}{v_t + v_p + v_{tp} + \dfrac{v_m + v_{tm} + v_e}{n}}$

where v_t, v_p, v_m and v_e represent the variance associated with topics, pupils, markers and error, respectively; v_{tp} and v_{tm} represent the variance associated with the interaction between topics and pupils, and topics and markers respectively.

Correlations (Part-Whole)

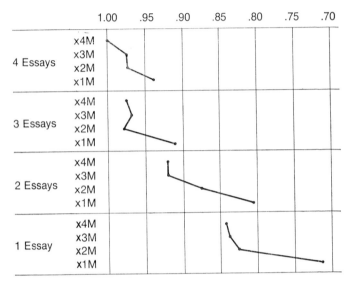

Figure 10.1 *Correlations between the Total of* 16 *Assessments* (4 × 4) *and Marks Obtained by Various Combinations of Essays and Markers*

The top half of Figure 10.1 shows consistently high correlations, indicating that an assessment based on three or four essays can produce a highly reliable result, and that little is gained by using more than one marker. Three essays and only one marker produce a total result slightly inferior to the others (0.91), and must be considered borderline. When only two essays are written, it requires three markers to gain the same borderline result (0.92). When fewer than three markers are used, on two essays, the correlations drop fast, from 0.92 down to 0.87 and 0.80.

Inspection of the bottom row of the table shows that one essay total provides a relatively unstable result, regardless of the number of markers. The pooling of results from two markers can compensate for the weakness of using only one marker, but there are diminishing returns for more than three. It would seem more profitable to have three or four essays, marked by one teacher, than one essay marked by three or four teachers.

These results confirm the conclusions drawn from the variance estimates obtained in the analysis of variance reported above. In assessing pupil ability in writing skill, the variation in pupil performance is a more serious matter than the variation between experienced, well-briefed markers. From the results of this chapter it seems that, to obtain an accurate estimate of pupils' writing skills, it is necessary to require them to write at least three essays, preferably four. If two markers are available, a reliable result can be obtained with three essays; if three markers are available, then two essays would suffice. Under no conditions can the assessment of a single essay be regarded as an adequate measure of writing skill no matter how many markers are used. The implications of this finding should be obvious, not only for research studies of this kind, but also for the reliability of 'one-shot' examinations in English. There is in these figures a clear case for requiring students to write on at least three and preferably four occasions in order to obtain a reliable index of their writing skill.

11

Conclusion

In his defence of the teaching of grammar, Gleason[1] argues that knowledge of grammar may result in 'an increased repertoire of choices, the addition of patterns and the clearer sensing of relations between patterns'. If it were true, this would make a study of grammar both useful and valid. On this assumption a student of grammar enhances his flexibility for framing his message to suit the occasion.

As we pointed out in Chapter 2, however, several generations of research have failed to reveal such benefits from grammar, and the experiment we have described, despite its extensive duration, its careful controls and the variety of criteria used, merely confirmed these earlier findings.

But Gleason went on to emphasize that the kind of grammar which is most likely to produce these literary advantages is 'the grammar that directs attention to sentence relations'. While there may be other grammars with such directive properties, the one which does it most conspicuously is transformational grammar. And the empirical studies of Bateman and Zidonis, and of Mellon, described in Chapter 2, provided strong hope that Gleason's claim had validity. Teachers who wanted their grammar to have pragmatic value, were given new faith.

Once again, the results of this study can only be regarded as unfulfilling. Transformational grammar, as represented in the Oregon Curriculum, seems to have no more effect on writing style, or on the variety in transformations used, or on conventional usage, than traditional grammar, or than no grammar at all. Whatever it takes to produce a competent writer, it seems that the knowledge and skill outcomes of a course in transformational grammar are neither necessary nor sufficient for this purpose.

1. H. A. Gleason, Jr., *Linguistics and English Grammar* (New York: Holt, Rinehart and Winston, 1965), p. 221.

The validity of these main conclusions depends, however, on the validity of the research procedures used. To aid the reader, a brief recapitulation is in order.

Summary

In the experiment we have described, three carefully matched groups of high school students studied three different English programmes for a period of three years. Two of the groups studied the Oregon Curriculum, one with, and the other without, the transformational grammar (TG) strand. The latter group substituted extra reading and creative writing for the TG strand. The third group of pupils studied a conventional English course, using P. R. Smart's textbook series *Let's Learn English* as a resource book. This series includes exercises in traditional grammar concepts, along with skill development in reading, writing, listening and speaking.

To minimize effects due to differences in the attitudes and competencies in the teachers, each English teacher taught each course, and the design of the study was such that in the course of the project, each class was taught for a year by each of the teachers. The pupils' language skills were compared at the end of each year of the project, that is, at the end of Forms 3, 4, and 5. A further follow-up comparison was made at the end of Form 6, 12 months after the experiment ceased. The measures used included essay writing (style, structure, mechanics, content), usage, sentence-combining, reading comprehension, vocabulary, literature, spelling, listening, variety of transformations, sentence structures, study skills, and attitudes towards various aspects of English.

All groups had approximately 574 periods of English in the three years, so distributed that each class had similar proportions of morning and afternoon periods, and of time spent on literature, composition and evaluation exercises. Teaching, marking and homework routines were standardized after regular consultation amongst the teachers. The teachers participating in the project were fully-qualified, experienced English teachers, who volunteered out of genuine interest in the outcome. All maintained an open mind about the results, before and after their reporting.

In the first two years of the study, no differences in language skills appeared between the three groups. At the end of the third year the groups were still very similar in the language tests and essay writing skills under study, and in their School Certificate English marks. Very small differences appeared in the usage exercises favouring the two grammar groups, but these were spread over a variety of test items, and could not have been predicted from an inspection of the skills developed in the grammar courses. Likewise, the two Oregon groups showed a marginally significant superiority ($F=3.23$, $p < 0.05$) over the LLE group in sentence-combining skills, but the differences were not readily

H

interpretable in curriculum terms, and were probably due to chance factors. The sixth form test of précis-writing skills, conducted 12 months after the experiment ended, confirmed the earlier findings, that there were no detectable differences between the three groups in language development.

Some differences did appear in the students' attitudes, particularly when assessed by the Semantic Differential procedure. The two grammar groups saw sentence-study as relatively 'useless', 'repetitive', and 'unpleasant', while the two Oregon groups showed marked positive feelings about literature and writing.

The latter finding has relevance for the more general evaluation, described in Chapter 9. The Oregon Curriculum does not stand or fall on the pragmatic value of its grammar course. As we noted earlier, the inclusion of this strand was justified by the authors on humanistic rather than utilitarian grounds. The subjective evaluation described in Chapter 8 shows that the teachers liked the course, for its organization, interest, and intellectual challenge, and the pupils clearly enjoyed the literature and rhetoric strands.

The LLE course was less favourably described by the teachers. As a resource series, it lacked the developmental sequence of the Oregon Curriculum, but positive comments were made of its variety of exercises, and particularly of its appealing material on the mass media.

Another incidental study was carried out to investigate the reliability of essay marking procedures. Correlational analyses and analyses of variance revealed that the day-to-day variability of pupil performance itself constituted a major source of unreliability in the assessment of writing skill. In the light of those studies it was recommended that formal assessments of pupils' writing ability should be spread over at least three occasions, and marked by two independent markers.

Discussion

The primary purpose of this investigation was to determine the direct effects of a study of transformational-generative grammar on the language growth of secondary school pupils. The results presented show that the effects of three years of such grammar study are negligible. Those pupils who studied no formal grammar for three years demonstrated competence in writing and related language skills equal to that shown by the pupils who studied transformational or traditional grammar. Furthermore, their attitude to English as a subject of study was more positive.

Proponents of grammar study may point out, of course, that the TG students did master the fundamentals of transformational grammar, without any apparent sacrifice in their language development, relative to the other students. Therefore this investigation could be said to provide little discomfort for those who support the study of grammar for its own sake or as a means of gaining a greater understanding of their language.

The nature and course of the language growth of these students was such that it was not seriously disadvantaged by a systematic study of grammar during the secondary school years. Moreover, it was the teachers' view that pupils could readily gain an understanding of basic concepts in transformational grammar in less than half the time; the concepts would be illustrated in fewer sentence types, but there would probably be an improvement in attitudes.

It is conceivable that a systematic study of grammar taught at a different level of the school might produce more obvious effects. As the writing style of the typical 13-year-old is probably less amenable to change than that of younger children, one might hypothesize that an earlier start in the primary school would be more profitable. Unfortunately, the essentially abstract nature of grammar makes such an hypothesis less credible. Certainly, teachers have succeeded in instructing primary school children in the exercise of sentence analysis, but in the light of research of Piaget and other developmental psychologists about the limited ability of pre-adolescent children to manipulate abstract concepts, it seems most unlikely that such training would be readily applied by children in their own writing. Furthermore, the researchers' empirical findings do not support an early introduction of grammar.

Perhaps then, the benefits to be derived from grammar are confined to bright children, those who can readily manipulate and apply those syntactic structures which they have studied. The subsidiary analyses conducted in the present investigation certainly did not show any important differences in the patterns of the above- and below-average pupils. It must be remembered, however, that the top-stream children (8-10 percent) had been deliberately omitted from the study. Curriculum planners should note, then, that the conclusions of the present investigation should be properly, if cautiously, restricted to typical secondary school pupils, and not to the brightest 10 percent. Nor can we generalize to older students, or, indeed, to learners of English as a second language.

What, traditionally, are the expected practical benefits of an effective course in English grammar? Defenders of the grammatical faith have emphasized the importance of sensitizing students to the variety of alternative ways of expressing an idea, to suit different occasions. The assumption is made that, by analysing the moveable parts and choice points in a sentence, and by rendering implicit habits explicit, pupils will consciously come to use a greater range of the structures they study, and to avoid inappropriate structures. However, it is highly debatable whether many students, or professional writers for that matter, are aware of the choices they make when generating new sentences. Habits of word production and sentence generation are set up very early in our language histories. Indeed the basic structures exist in most children's repertoire during their primary school days and seem to be relatively impervious to influence from analytic and somewhat unexciting written exercises. It may be true that new constructions can be taught to English pupils, but there is neither empirical nor theoretical justification for the teaching of current grammars for this purpose.

Some would argue that an understanding of grammar is needed before one can successfully undertake the editing of written prose. Amongst other things the good editor is expected to identify inappropriate sentence structures, and to reconstruct them without changing the meaning of the sentence. If, indeed, a study of grammar produces such a linguistic ability (which may not be reflected in writing performance), we would have expected it to show up in the tests of sentence-combining where the students had to modify sentences in just such a way. But the non-grammar groups achieved just as well as, or better than, the other groups on this exercise. And even if a knowledge of grammar did some day prove to be a pre-requisite for editorial tasks, it would need more justification than this to be seen as essential study for the general run of the high school population.

Meanwhile, given that grammar has a negligible influence on children's language growth, it still requires a deliberate value judgement to decide whether to include or exclude it from the English programme. Lovers of English language may well continue to justify its instruction on humanistic grounds. Thus, Paul Roberts[2] claims that language should be studied 'objectively and dispassionately, for its own sake', whereas Peter Rosenbaum points out that the student of linguistics 'is involving himself in a study which has had intrinsic intellectual appeal for centuries, the study of those abilities which make human beings human'.[3]

The more pragmatic English teacher will doubtless reject this argument, and point to the increasing congestion of the secondary school curriculum and the negative attitudes that grammar study frequently engenders. There are today so many calls on the students' time that there is need for more convincing reasons to justify the presence of grammar in a crowded curriculum.

The implication of the 'grammar for its own sake' argument is that no better rationale exists. It is surely time for those who support grammar to spell out more forcibly its 'humane' benefits, and to identify the contexts in which it might best be taught—When? To whom? To what end?

At this point, it is appropriate to explore further the question of whether the study of grammar is an expensive luxury. The present study showed neither advantage nor disadvantage in language growth relative to the other groups. But there is a disquieting suspicion in the results, that none of the groups made substantial gains in writing skill, with or without grammar.

Many of the students who participated in this investigation showed considerable skill in writing at the outset. It was noticeable, however, that those students whose writing was highly rated in the third form, were still the best writers in the fifth form. When a comparative analysis was made of third and fifth form essays, written on the same topics and marked

2. P. Roberts, 'The Relation of Linguistics to the Teaching of English', in *College English*, No. 22, pp. 7–8, 1960.

3. P. Rosenbaum, 'On the Role of Linguistics in the Teaching of English', in *Harvard Educational Review*, Vol. 35, No. 3, p. 341, 1965.

'blind', the correlation between the marks on both occasions was almost 0.5, a relatively high figure considering the unreliability of marking. The good writers stayed good; the poor improved but little. More important, they all showed only a modest growth in written composition skills over the two year period. The actual mean gain was only 2.92 (out of 32 points), or 60 percent of one standard deviation. The increase was statistically significant, but by no means reassuring. So, whatever the components of an effective writing programme in the secondary school may be, it seems unlikely that the three courses studied in this project have produced a formula for dramatic improvement. The fifth formers were writing with little more control or fluency and with the same kinds of sentence structures as they used in the third form. In the light of this finding, it is not sufficient to claim that the grammar students did not sacrifice any language growth, relative to the others. It seems that grammar has no practical benefits in an absolute sense. And we cannot ignore the negative feelings the grammar students showed at the end of the experiment.

The present study was evaluative rather than exploratory in its intentions. Therefore, no clear recommendations can be made about the kind of programme which might have a striking impact on the composition skills of secondary school pupils. Such a research exercise would seem to require either a more intensive, longitudinal study of the writing development of individual children, or a programme developed from a completely new set of theoretical proposals about the nature of children's language growth. The time is clearly ripe for more experiment with other approaches to the teaching of English, such as the kind of naturalistic language curricula being advocated by the New English Syllabus Committee in New Zealand and the National Council of Teachers of English in the USA.

Appendix 1

NOTES FOR ESSAY MARKERS, 1971

Most teachers are aware of the difficulty of making a reliable assessment of writing ability. Our thinking has been guided by conversations and correspondence with NZCER staff and by two American publications: *Research in Written Composition* by Braddock, Lloyd-Jones and Schoer (NCTE, Illinois, 1963) and *The Measurement of Writing Ability* by Godshalk, Swineford and Coffman (College Entrance Examination Board, New York 1966).

The Problem

Many factors interfere with the accurate assessment of writing ability. The following outline is derived mainly from Braddock et al.

1. *Writer Variables*
    (a) A writer's performance differs from day to day and from time to time within the day. Godshalk et al. found the variation especially pronounced in the performance of better writers.
    (b) A writer's performance differs from topic to topic. Giving pupils a choice of topics is no solution because there is no evidence that they choose the best topic for themselves.

2. *Topic Variable*
Some topics are more difficult to write on than others; expository topics may be more difficult than narrative or descriptive topics.

3. *Marker Variables*
    (a) The marker's personal feelings influence his mark. He may react more sympathetically to girls than to boys or favour Polynesians above Pakehas (Europeans). If the marker believes that grammar should be taught, he may be generous to members of a class which he knows has been taught

grammar. Even if he is aware of his sympathy, any knowledge of the origin of the script will influence his assessment.

(b) Markers are generally more generous at the beginning of a marking period than they are at the end. When markers are tired they become more severe, more lenient or more erratic. Good or bad handwriting and few or excessive mechanical errors tend to have a halo effect at the best of times. This effect becomes more pronounced in tired markers.

(c) As well as being lenient or harsh by nature, different people value different aspects of essay writing more than others. Freedom from mechanical errors is valued most highly by some people, an individual style by others, original ideas by a third group, and so on. This is perhaps the most difficult variable to control.

Thus we can see that the mark given to one piece of writing by a single marker can depend more on the time of the week or day it was written, the pupil's choice of topic, the marker's attitude to, say, the emancipation of women, the time of day at which he marked it, and the set of writing values he has, than it does on the actual writing ability of the pupil.

Why Try to Mark Essays at All?

The College Entrance Examinations Board in the United States abandoned essays for a time, measuring associated skills—like mechanical correctness and ability in organizing ideas—by objective tests. But there is more to effective writing than avoiding gross errors. The truly effective writer has an individual style, chooses appropriate words, communicates ideas and impressions, moves his reader to sympathy with him. These things can be tested only by essay writing. Our research aims to investigate the effect on writing skills of spending a third of teaching time on a study of TG grammar, and it is therefore essential for us to have our classes write essays, and to have them marked as accurately as possible.

An Attempt to Control the Variables

1. *Writer and Topic Variables*
The research group wrote three essays over a period of four weeks on topics which were pretested to ensure that they produced three different types of writing. In 1970 our pupils wrote four essays, but it was found that dropping one essay did not affect accuracy of assessment. No choice of topics was given.

2. *Marker Variables*
Pupils were numbered at random and only their numbers appear on the essays, so that markers know as little as possible about individuals and their English classes. The scripts will be arranged so that no pupil will have all his essays marked at the beginning or at the end of a session. We hope that the marking load for each individual is reasonable, and that there will be enough rest periods to reduce marker fatigue.

How can markers' differing views of what constitutes writing excellence be controlled? The most generally accepted methods are either impressionistic or analytic in approach.

In the impressionistic method, markers read the essay rapidly once, and write down a mark. They use their own judgement entirely. Scores from several independent readings are totalled to reach the final mark for each piece of writing. The marker variable is reduced by allowing markers' idiosyncracies to balance each other out. Writer variables are reduced by having students write more than one essay. Godshalk et al. found that the total mark became more reliable as the number of different pieces written by each pupil, and the number of independent readings of them, increased. Five essays, each one read by five markers, produced as high a figure for reliability as could be expected in the measurement of writing ability.

Although this method is very reliable and easy to organize, we felt that something would be lost if we used this method for evaluating our research essays. We would end up with a reliable total mark for our essays. There might be no significant difference between the performance of the RW, TG and LLE groups on this figure. But there might remain unrevealed interesting and significant differences between the groups' performances in different aspects of essay writing. It is possible, for example, that the RW group, having spent one third of its time in extra reading and writing, will have developed more ideas than the TG group. The TG group may construct sentences more fluently. We therefore decided to adopt an analytic method of marking.

An analytic method aims to control the marker variable by isolating separate aspects of essay writing and directing the marker's attention equally to all of them. This means that his personal emphasis cannot influence the total score, which is calculated from the separate marks given for each aspect. Even if he does regard style, for example, as most important, he has to give content and organization equal attention. Some preparation and practice for markers is necessary in an analytic method to establish a common understanding of the requirements of each criterion.

In devising our analytic method of marking we have tried to incorporate the advantages of an impressionistic method by asking markers to read essays impressionistically on the criteria of content, organization, style and mechanics. This enables rapid readings to be made, and by totalling several markers' scores we hope to balance differences within each criterion. Last year we had pupils write four essays, and each essay was read by four markers. An analysis of those results showed, however, that three essays read by two markers would provide practically as reliable a score, and we have modified our procedure accordingly.

This is the way we have planned the marking. The essays will be marked title by title in three sessions on Wednesday, Thursday and Friday, 1, 2, and 3 December. Because we found last year that the criteria revealed themselves differently in each title, test essays will be marked and discussed at the beginning of each session. Markers will be divided into three teams. The essays, in groups of 16, will be moved from marker to marker so that every essay is read twice by different markers, and so that all markers read at least one example of each pupil's work. We suggest that each group of essays be marked in the same way as they were in 1970. Each essay in the group is read first for content, and its score on a four-point scale entered on the mark sheet. The marker then returns to the first essay in the group, and re-reads each one for organization. He does the same for each criterion. What we are after is a rapid, concentrated reading with the requirements of the criterion firmly in mind to produce a clear impression of the essay's worth on that criterion, rather than a mechanical count of any sort. We think that separate readings are necessary to avoid the halo effect mentioned earlier; we want to make sure as far as possible that performance in an area does not influence the mark given in another area. To help achieve this independence we have organized the mark sheets so that, when the score on each criterion is entered, the scores on other criteria are out of sight. We hope that the groups of essays are large enough for each assessment to be made separately, and yet small enough for the second, third and fourth readings to be much quicker than the first. To ensure that markers make an independent assessment of each essay, we would ask that essays are not discussed until both readings have been completed.

We have chosen a four-point scale as Godshalk et al. found this produced the best results. They found that it forced markers to a decision; it did not allow them to take a middle mark if they were in doubt. It is important to use all the points of the scale and to aim to give the same number of marks on the top half of the scale in each criterion as you do on the bottom half. There should be about the same number of 1s and 2s as there are 3s and 4s. This may be difficult with these fourth form essays, but we are trying to rate them in relation to each other and not against an absolute standard.

The Criteria

Content
Incidents. Generalizations. Details supporting generalizations. Choice of material to fulfil the purpose of the essay. Relevance of ideas to the topic.

Organization
Logical development, sentence by sentence, paragraph by paragraph.
Organization of material for best effect.
Is it possible to state clearly the central idea of the essay?

Style
Involvement of audience.
Awareness of audience and purpose in appropriate word choice and register
Is the point of view consistent and appropriate?
Originality and vividness of word choice.
Appropriateness of sentence patterns (variety, or repetition for effect).
Control over tense.

Mechanics
Repeated errors, rather than obvious carelessness.
Punctuation, spelling, use of conventions such as indentation of paragraphs.
Grammatical correctness (not to be confused with appropriate register in style).

Appendix 2

TEST OF PHRASE STRUCTURE AND TRANSFORMATION RULES—FORM 5, 1972

At the end of Form 5, the TG pupils were given a test to assess their ability to analyse typical sentences, using phrase structure and transformation rules. Each class was given the same set of 4 or 5 sentences involving different structures. This is an example: *Ross, a bird fancier, races pigeons.*

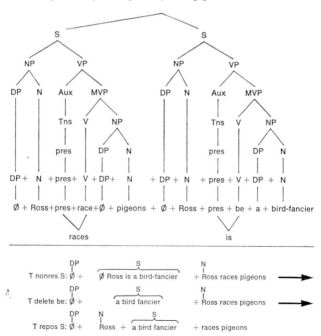

Results

36% completed the exercise with no error at all.

15% made one slight error probably due to carelessness or poor setting out (e.g., writing N for NP or vice versa, or failing to carry parts of the symbol string down to the sentence string).

19% made two or three such slight errors.

24% made one major error (e.g., incorrect transformation, dominant sentence embedded in subordinate sentence) in one sentence, but were correct in the other sentences.

6% did not achieve any full, correct sentence.

It can thus be concluded that 94% of the TG students were largely correct in their description of most sentences, and had therefore acquired an adequate grasp of concepts which were taught in the course.

Index

PRINTED BY WHITCOULLS LIMITED—G16068